THE CATS OF AFRICA

THE CATS OF AFRICA

PHOTOGRAPHS BY **JOHN DOMINIS** TEXT BY **MAITLAND EDEY**

TIME-LIFE BOOKS NEW YORK

CONTENTS

I am not a specialist in wild animal photography; rather I am a professional photo-journalist, and when the Editors of LIFE asked me to photograph the cats of Africa, I started thinking about this assignment in the same way that I would have about any other photographic essay. That is, rather than go for portraits of various animals, I wanted as much as possible to make a series of pictures that would show how these animals live and what they are like, as one would do a picture story on a human personality. Therefore I needed the cats in action, doing what they normally do. I decided to use only natural light to eliminate any artificial quality to the photographs.

The first thing I learned was that I was going to miss many more pictures than I was going to get. Although previous experience in sports photography helped me to react quickly, many many times while I was photographing the cats interesting things would happen too far away even for long telephoto lenses, or behind bushes and trees, or when it was too dark. Some pictures were spoiled simply by the harsh midday light. Light is a crucial element in photography, and although it cannot be controlled in animal photography, it can be exploited. Quite a bit can be done with back lighting and the warm beauty of dawn and dusk.

I talked myself into not worrying about the pictures that I missed, and made certain that the ones I did get would be good. I spent nine months in Africa on this job, and except for making plans, testing equipment, buying supplies, hiring people and repairing vehicles, I spent every day in the field from before dawn until after dusk. I believe that you must find an animal or a pride first thing in the morning and stay with it all day, never leaving to go back to camp for a beer because that is just when something will happen. With a lot of time, a lot of patience, a very large portion of luck, some good camera equipment and a little ability, good pictures can be made in the wild.

Gradually, I learned more about the habits of the cats, and could anticipate what they might do, and this helped me to be ready with the right camera and lens at the right time. Sometimes I could arrange matters to improve my chances. Of course I got a lot of help and advice from the game wardens and rangers in all the game reserves and parks in Kenya, Tanzania, Rhodesia, South Africa and Botswana. These men were uniformly cooperative. I am particularly grateful to Simon Tippis, the warden of Kekorok. I would also like to mention Simon Trevor, who spent a great deal of time with me in the field as co-camper, game scout and constant adviser. Finally, my thanks to John Mbotu, my driver and all-round helper, an endlessly cheerful and resourceful man.

Many professional hunters and local photographers were also very helpful during my stay in Africa, but I must say that just when we would think that we knew these cats so well that we could prejudge their moves, they would do something just the opposite and against all the rules. I've seen lions hunt downwind, which any Boy Scout knows you shouldn't do. And I've seen lions and cheetahs mess up their attempts to kill dozens of times more often than I saw them make a successful kill. I don't give the big cats credit for being superbly intelligent and cunning, as do some animal lovers, but I do like them and respect them.

For two of the species of cats that I was interested in, the problem of lighting was easy. Lions, in areas where they are not hunted, are conspicuous and fearless animals. They live their lives out in the open and conduct many of their affairs during the day. You have only to find them and stick with them. Most of the time they will ignore you completely, and you can work as close to them as you like, so long as you stay in a vehicle. Contrary to popular belief, they do hunt quite often in the daytime. Hanging around lions is a pure delight, and the temptation is to spend too much of your time with them at the expense of the harder work you know you will have to put in on some of the more elusive species. All the lion pictures in this book were of wild individuals. They were taken in Wankie, Rhodesia; on the Serengeti Plain; and in Kekorok and Amboseli, Kenya.

Next easiest of the cats to photograph are cheetahs. They are also diurnal, but they are much scarcer than lions. An added problem is that they run down their prey rather than stalking and pouncing on it. This means that they range fast and far, and your chance of being up close for a cheetah kill is poor. Furthermore, if you try to overcome this by sticking too close to the hunting animal, you destroy *his* chances. Follow him around all day, and he may get nothing. Persist in this, and you may drive him to starvation.

Luckily, cheetahs are easily tamed. Even more luckily, tame ones behave in the field just as wild ones do. The best picture I got of a cheetah chasing game *(pages 140-141)* was of a tame animal. One other picture of that same animal is on pages 138-139. All the other cheetah pictures in this book are of wild animals living in Amboseli and Nairobi Parks. I stress this point because cheetahs normally travel singly or in pairs, and some sharp-eyed reader may wonder how groups of three, four and five adults were seen together, if they were not tame animals assembled for the sake of a good picture. The answer is that the group pictures are of families. The youngsters had grown as large as their mother but had not yet left home.

For a natural-light photographer the really impossible animal is the leopard. Leopards are solitary, hard to find, afraid of man and usually nocturnal in their hunting habits. Action pictures of leopards are ordinarily made with baited carcasses triggered to flash or strobe units. I did not want pictures of this kind, and I solved the problem as best I could by locating a man who had several captive leopards. I made an arrangement with him by which we would truck the leopards out to where we had previously made sure game would be, turn the leopards loose and hope for the best.

The pictures on pages 110-117 were taken under these conditions in the Kalahari Desert, Botswana. The action was unpredictable and very swift. To get anything at all I had to use a hand-held, motor driven camera set to take a picture every third of a second. On one occasion a baboon ran right through the flat-bed truck from which I was working, closely followed by a leopard which actually went between my legs.

This was the only phase of the assignment I did not enjoy, because I was frankly afraid of the leopards. "Tameness" is a relative matter with these animals. A few years before, one of the leopards we were working with had clawed off the scalp and nearly killed the teen-age daughter of the man who owned it—pouncing instinctively in reaction to some inadvertent movement of hers. I never turned my back on those leopards and was thankful when the job was over. I made one picture in the Pretoria Zoo of a black leopard because they are so rare, and finding one in the wild would have been next to impossible. This is one place where I broke my own rule and used electronic flash to light him.

The two smaller cats, the serval and caracal, presented still another problem. They are extremely shy, and are almost never seen. You *must* find an animal that is used to people if you expect to get any pictures at all. Domestication has little or no effect on their behavior in the field. Like house cats, they do their stalking and pouncing whether you are standing by with a camera or not.

The serval pictures are of an extremely friendly animal belonging to Bobbie Cade of Nairobi. Cade runs an "orphanage" for strays and cripples and abandoned young of all species that are turned in at the Nairobi National Park. He obtained his serval that way. It was accustomed to humans and made its marvelous bounding leaps in the tall grass utterly oblivious of my presence.

The caracal was more difficult. Although a captive animal, it was completely wild and could not be approached, let alone touched. We put it in a large enclosure to prevent its escaping altogether. This simulated its natural habitat, being full of trees and undergrowth. The caracal was often hard to find in there, and had to be stalked with great care and circumspection; otherwise it would simply hide in deeper bush. It always snarled viciously when I approached too close to it. This reaction is clearly shown in the picture on page 176.

For those interested in equipment, a few words on that. I bought a Toyota Land Cruiser, which performed beautifully over the worst country. A hole was cut in the top, allowing me to stand inside the vehicle and operate cameras through this hatch. On top I mounted a Miller tripod head and attached a Nikon camera with motor drive and a 600mm Nikon lens to it. In addition I held, or had close at hand, three more motor-driven Nikons with 300mm, 135mm and 50mm lenses. Thus equipped, I was well prepared for things happening at different distances. Of course, I was caught with the wrong camera in my hands during some action, and a few times I was forced simply to drop a camera on the ground in order to grab another with the right lens, focus, and shoot. This had to be done within a second or two or the picture would have been gone. The motorized Nikon allows shooting three pictures a second without winding, so you have more chances of catching the action at its peak, plus the possibility of making an entire sequence of an event. I had two or three spare Nikons back in Nairobi to replace those that I repeatedly broke through my rough handling of them. This may seem like unnecessarily brutal treatment of delicate equipment, but it can't be avoided if you do not want to miss pictures. Contrary to most advice, I did not keep the cameras in cases to prevent dust from covering them. Dust is not good for cameras, but a clean camera isn't worth much if you can't use it when you need it.

I used Ektachrome X film throughout. Despite the small 35mm size I used, it served me well. Many game photographers prefer larger cameras and a larger film size in order to get finer detail on their negatives, particularly if they plan to enlarge them, but I find the 35mm quality adequate. I also find the larger cameras too slow and clumsy for really fast shooting.

JOHN DOMINIS

AN INTRODUCTION TO THE CATS

For a proper appreciation of the cats of Africa, the reader should know something about cats in general: what they are like, what kinds of cats there are scattered around the world, how there was a time on this earth when no cats existed anywhere. Therefore, this book will begin with what makes a cat a cat. And if it seems to wander off along the way into discussion of dogs, seals and woodchucks, it will get back to cats in due course.

A convenient place to start is with a look at the common house cat. Nine people out of 10 would probably describe this familiar animal as a rather smallish four-legged creature with thick soft fur, large eyes, erect, pointed ears, sharp teeth, sharp claws and a long tail. One might go on to say that it has excellent hearing, a good sense of smell, is warm-blooded, suckles its young and can make a variety of noises to express itself.

Very good. Unfortunately, however, these characteristics are also just as descriptive of the family dog. If by chance, he is a mutt—perhaps a cross between a fox terrier and a cocker spaniel—then he too is rather small; his coat, if not as thick as a cat's, is nevertheless thick and silky; his eyes are large; his ears stick up; his tail is long; his teeth, although not of the needle sharpness of a cat's, are still good and sharp. He too is warm-blooded, and has a keen nose and ears. He makes a variety of interesting noises and, like a cat, was once nursed by his mother.

There must be something wrong here; we started to describe a cat and ended up with a description of a dog! Although any child can tell the difference between a cat and a dog, describing those differences is not so easy because their similarities are far greater than their differences. To get a useful description of a cat, one's observations must be more sophisticated. Therefore, it may help to start again by disposing of the similarities—by announcing that a cat is a mammalian carnivore, a meat-eater, which right away explains its resemblance to dogs, otters, weasels and a large variety of other mammals that live by hunting. They all have sharp teeth, furry

coats, etc. Some, it is true, do not look much like cats. A seal, for example, is also a carnivore, but it adapted ages ago to life in cold water—its
body torpedo-shaped and its legs and feet modified into flippers for swim-
ming instead of running.

Seal and cat are much more closely related than they seem. Each lives
on raw meat that it must catch by its own efforts. This is one of the ancestral habits that link them, wildly different though they may look—far
more different than, say, a cat and a woodchuck. A woodchuck is about
the same size, and about the same shape and color as a house cat, and if
one were to see a small grayish-brown animal sitting quietly in the grass behind the barn some evening when the light was beginning to go, he might
not be able to tell which it was—cat or woodchuck.

But as soon as it moved one would know; a woodchuck hunches cautiously along, nibbling grasses and herbs. It is in its behavior, personality,
character (whatever we choose to call it) that the lowly stolid woodchuck re-
veals himself as a woodchuck, a world apart from the lithe, resourceful
and altogether captivating mixture of body and behavior that go to make
up a cat. No woodchuck ever strolled out of an evening, head high, tail higher, lord of all he surveyed. One need only watch the two in action for a
moment to realize that any cat is much more interesting and much smarter than any woodchuck.

All carnivores are intelligent. They have to be. A fundamental of their existence is that they be smarter than the animals they hunt, or they would
soon all starve to death. A woodchuck may be a very paragon of circumspection, listening cautiously and looking carefully around before he
comes out of his burrow, alert to any strange shadow or movement, seldom straying more than a few feet from safety. Nevertheless, there may
be a fox or bobcat in the neighborhood. If so, it will have the wit and patience to break down those defenses. It will study the terrain and the
direction of the wind, hide in a good spot, hold still for an hour if necessary, judge the distance from which it can effectively spring and time its
pounce just right. Before too long the bobcat will be dining on woodchuck.

This is not to play down the woodchuck. What he is designed to do he
does very well. He is a determined digger, a lusty reproducer of his own
kind, a creature of perpetual and admirable timidity and such a frugal con-
servator of his own bodily fuels that he can sleep the winter away without
eating at all. When spring comes and he is hungry again, he can wax fat
on a profusion of foods that grow all around his doorstep. In fact, his life
is so logical and simple that one may be tempted to ask how it is that preda-

tors ever came into being at all. Why, if grass is so green and so abundant, did animals ever evolve that were put to the much more arduous necessity of killing other animals to survive?

This is an interesting question, and worth a short digression into the subject of evolution, for meat-eating as a way of life was invented long before mammals were. It was honorably practiced by their ancestors the reptiles, by *their* ancestors the amphibians, by *their* ancestors the fishes, and so on, back down the misty evolutionary trail as far as one cares to trace the habit. It seems there have always been plant-eaters and flesh-eaters. This being so, it is tempting to select a placid slow-moving grass-eating, heavy-footed, meadow-dwelling, cow-sized reptile, and wonder if it was not the ancestor of the modern cow.

The answer is an emphatic no. Evolution did not work that way at all. The scientists who have been sorting out old bones and arranging them into sense-making relationships quickly discovered that cows are not descended from herbivorous cowlike reptiles but from predatory little lizardlike reptiles. It is from these creatures that all mammals are descended. Cows got to be like cows, cats like cats, *after* they became mammals, not before.

The changeover from reptiles to mammals was a gradual one. It took place in a group of small and inconspicuous reptiles some time between 190 and 250 million years ago. In the process there was a long period during which these little creatures were neither reptile nor mammal but something in-between.

Major transformations do not take place overnight, and there were animals hanging about for millions of years that had confusing mixtures of reptilian and mammalian traits. If someone were to take a cube of wood and once a year give one of its corners a rub with a silk handkerchief, after an eon or so he would have succeeded in turning that cube into a round wooden ball, but there would be a considerable period in-between when it was neither ball nor cube.

Ultimately the cube did become a ball. The rubbing of time rounded off the corners and produced something that any expert would agree was no longer a reptile but an honest-to-goodness mammal. It was not much to look at. It was about the size of a rat, and had a vaguely ratlike or weasellike shape to it. It was neither a plant-eater nor was it a true carnivore. It lived almost entirely on insects.

Improbable as it may seem, cows and cats, hippopotamuses and gorillas are all descended from those early insect-eaters. To understand how these astonishing changes came about, it may be helpful to return to the woodchuck again. Let us make some possibly ridiculous assumptions and picture him comfortably established in the state of Connecticut, as he is today, but let us make one radical change in his living condition. Let us assume that he is the only mammal found in Connecticut. There are no skunks around, no rabbits, no mice, no foxes, no deer, not even any human beings to make trouble—only woodchucks.

In a situation like that, with nothing to bother them, it is clear that there soon would be a great many woodchucks and that the principal problem encountered by any single woodchuck would be other woodchucks. The others would eat his food, dig their holes where he wanted to dig, run off with female woodchucks that he wanted for himself. At that point slight differences between woodchucks would begin to be very important. Those that were bigger, stronger and more aggressive might be able to chase others away from their own patches of grass. When the competition for dwindling supplies of food began to get really serious, those bigger tougher woodchucks would be the ones that survived. They would be the ones that would live to mate and reproduce others like them. And if large size and aggressive behavior were really helpful, those attributes would become increasingly concentrated. In time, a brand of woodchuck might emerge that was 10 or 20 times as large as the one we know today.

But what about all the other ordinary meek little woodchucks? Would they be crowded out by the big ones and become extinct? They might. But depending on luck and circumstances, a great many other things might happen to them.

A few, driven by hunger, might eke out their diet by eating bark, or some other material that woodchucks do not usually eat. Those that could digest bark the best would again be the survivors, and in due course there might evolve a race of bark-eating woodchucks that no longer would—or even could—eat grass. In order to scramble high into the trees to reach tender young bark, those with the most flexible legs and the strongest claws would be favored. Ultimately there might evolve a kind of tree-climbing woodchuck, one that found life in the branches so comfortable that it never came to the ground at all.

Still others, unable to stomach bark, might discover that they could survive by hanging around as scavengers. The skinniest and speediest among them could sneak in, grab a few bites of grass and scamper off before the slower, hulking proprietors of the grass plots could catch them. Better yet, they might concentrate on certain plants that the big grass-eaters did not care for. In time a small plant-eater and a big grass-eater might discover that they could live side by side without bothering each other at all.

Finally there might be a pioneer or two that, grubbing around among the roots and dead leaves, decided to fill up on bugs or worms. After a few hundred thousand years of this there might evolve woodchucks that lived exclusively on bugs and worms. The largest and most agile of these could conceivably graduate to frogs, and from eating frogs it is only a small step to eating small woodchucks.

Ridiculous? Perhaps. But if for the overgrown grass-eating woodchuck we substitute the word buffalo, if we call the bark-eater a porcupine, the scavenger a sheep, and the frog-eater a lion, then we have a highly simplified picture of what actually did happen to the mammals. Instead of starting off as woodchucks, they started off as something just as unpromising —those little insectivores already mentioned—but somehow they did manage to turn themselves into the four thousand different kinds of mammals that inhabit the earth today, not to mention a much larger number that also developed but that have since become extinct.

This, in a nutshell, is what evolution is all about. Animals are fantastically adaptable. Their bodies and behavior, thanks to differences in their genetic makeup, are almost unbelievably plastic. Given enough time, and the opportunity to flow imperceptibly toward another way of life that seems to offer slightly better chances than the one now being led, animals will change. The world offers a wide variety of environmental niches for pioneering creatures to fill, and they have been filling them in a steady stream. There are more different kinds of living things on earth today than there were 50 million years ago, and a great many more than there were 500 million years ago. The reason is that the very branching out and filling of niches creates new niches. There could be no such thing as bees until flowers had made their appearance. Now there are birds called bee-eaters. There are also bee-eater-eaters, better known as hawks.

So, back to cats. As stated, they, along with all other mammals, are descended from small insectivorous warm-blooded creatures that first made their appearance about 190 million years ago. Things moved slowly in those days, and it was not until about 130 million years later that the descendants of those original insectivores began to show characteristics in some of their lines that would lead to the animals we know today. One such line starts with a small group of animals called miacids, and they were the ancestors of all living carnivores. They, like their ancestral insect-eaters, were generally small, long-bodied, short-legged and had long narrow snouts. However, they had made the jump from eating insects to larger prey. In addition, their skulls were roomier, and it is believed that their brains were considerably more complex. All in all, the miacids can be regarded as a kind of general utility-model carnivore, efficient but unspecialized. And the model has survived in a few groups with only slight modifications right down to today. There is a family of carnivores named viverrids that are widely spread through Eurasia and Africa. One member, the genet, is often seen in forests around the Mediterranean, and anybody wishing to know what the original meat-eating ancestor of all the cats looked like could scarcely do better than take a good look at a genet.

What happened to the miacids? They simply obliterated themselves by evolving into other things at a bewildering rate. The times were propitious for such an explosion. The great age of reptiles had come to a close; the dinosaurs were gone, and there were many inviting niches wide open for enterprising carnivores to flow into and grow into. The chart opposite shows how they took advantage of that golden opportunity. During a mere 40 million years they developed into 10 distinct families of meat-eaters, some of them with characteristics so unusual that no one could have seriously considered the possibility of their developing—except that they did. Three of those families—the seals, sea lions and walruses—moved back to the sea. Of these the walruses are perhaps the most unusual. These huge arctic animals make their living by diving down and digging mollusks from the bottom of the ocean with their tusk-like canine teeth, which sometimes grow over three feet long. A walrus tusk is about as long as its entire miacid ancestor. It is almost inconceivable that one should be descended from the other.

Of the seven families of land carnivores, none took such bizarre turns as the seagoing ones. In fact the majority of the land carnivores, compared with many other mammals, are not particularly specialized. Why should they be, when the generalized form of the first carnivore was a good one? Presumably it could see, hear and smell well. It could run fast and was reasonably strong and tough for its size. Furthermore, the food that it ate—meat—was not only the richest and most concentrated stuff available, but it could be quickly converted into energy and tissue by a relatively simple digestive mechanism. Basically, what modern dogs and cats have achieved is improvement of the characteristics that their ancestors already had; they are swifter, stronger, keener-eyed and more acute in nose and ear—but otherwise not too different.

Evolution has produced 10 families of mammalian carnivores, all descended from a single ancestral group, the miacids, who lived 50 or 60 million years ago. These animals were about two feet long, weighed about 10 pounds and were proportioned very much as shown in the drawing opposite. Whether they were striped or spotted, or indeed if they had any marks at all, is not known. However, their descendants tend to have certain markings in common, and the best guess is that the miacids were striped or spotted with a pattern not unlike that of today's tabby.

Not enough fossils have been recovered to say precisely how the subsequent radiation of the carnivores took place (*dotted lines*), but within about 10 million years nine distinct families had emerged. One other—the hyenas—came along more recently. Each of these families has since subdivided into many species (see *figures at top of chart*), each specialized to fit a particular niche. Surrounded by these increasingly efficient animals, and presumably no longer able to compete with them, the miacid group became extinct four million years ago.

THE EVOLUTION OF THE CARNIVORES

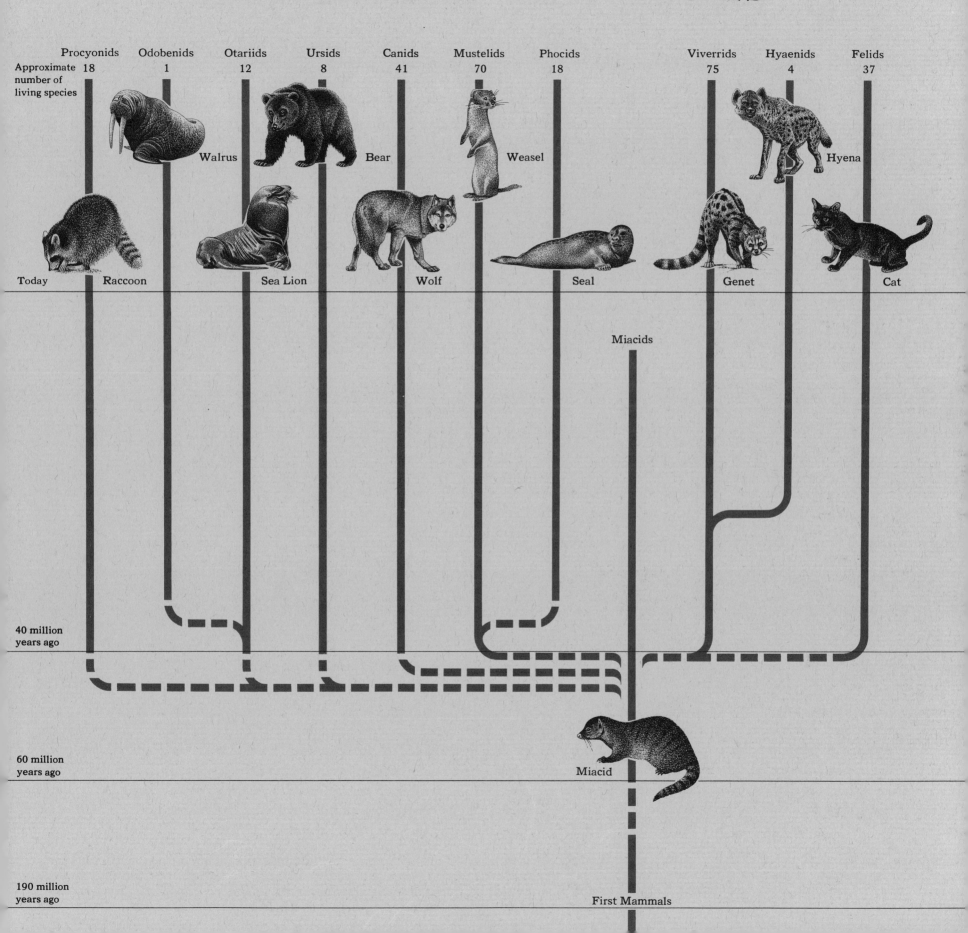

Procyonids 18   Odobenids 1   Otariids 12   Ursids 8   Canids 41   Mustelids 70   Phocids 18   Viverrids 75   Hyaenids 4   Felids 37

Approximate number of living species

Walrus   Bear   Weasel   Hyena

Today   Raccoon   Sea Lion   Wolf   Seal   Genet   Cat

Miacids

40 million years ago

60 million years ago   Miacid

190 million years ago   First Mammals

By contrast, the evolution of a cow has been spectacular. It has traveled a far greater distance from the ancestral insect-eating mammals than the carnivores have. The arrangement and proportions of a cow's bones have been radically altered. From somewhere or other it has produced a large set of horns. Its functional toes have been reduced from five to two, and its hoof now consists largely of a pair of oversized toenails. In order to digest grass and hay instead of insects, it has a much more complicated digestive system and must spend a good deal of its time regurgitating the food it has eaten in order to chew it over a second time. Clearly the vegetable-eating way of life is not quite as easy as it might at first seem.

The cats have not had to undergo such radical changes. To bring down a zebra requires a large killer like a lion; to bring down a mouse requires a small one like a house cat, but the model is essentially the same. Nevertheless there *are* differences among carnivores—between dog and cat— and a good place to begin examining them is in the head.

A cat's head is much rounder than a dog's. It is wider, and the nose and jaw are much shorter. What is the reason for this difference in head shape? The principal one given by many authorities is that the dog's nose is all-important to it in hunting. A cat has a good sense of smell, but it is nothing like as keen as a dog's. A cat relies more on sight and hearing and, surprisingly, on touch—which accounts for another cat characteristic, those magnificent whiskers that it wears. Cats do much of their hunting at night, and whiskers enable them to move quietly through dense cover, feeling their way as they go, aware of the exact location of twigs and leaves, which they are able to touch without disturbing. A cat's whisker is fairly stiff and strong at its base, but it tapers to a marvelously fine and flexible end. The most conspicuous whiskers spring out sideways in a noble spray from each upper lip, but many cats also have several long tactile hairs growing upward and forward from the eyebrows.

Another reason for the greater length of a dog's muzzle is that it must accommodate more teeth than a cat's. And these teeth must do more things. Both animals have large well-developed canines for fighting, biting and killing as well as other teeth called carnassials that have a shearing effect when lower jaw meets upper, enabling the user to tear hunks of meat from a carcass. It is in the molars farther back in the jaw that the dog is better endowed. Somewhere along the line, the cat's ancestors lost some of these, which is not surprising because a molar is for grinding, and a cat does not grind. Cats chew scarcely at all. As soon as they succeed in getting a manageable piece of meat into the mouth they swallow it. They never grind up bones as a dog does; they cannot. A cat's jaw works only in two directions: up and down. To grind, one must also be able to move the jaw sideways, as dogs—and humans—do.

Another important factor in the flatness of the cat's face is that it depends on its eyes more than a dog does. Since both are hunting animals and must be able to judge distances of moving prey precisely, their eyes face forward rather than to the side. This means that the field of view of each eye overlaps that of the other, providing what is known as binocular vision, and thus giving extremely good depth perception. Herbivores do not need binocular vision; their food is standing still. What they do need is to be able to see potential enemies coming from any direction. Consequently their eyes are on the sides of their heads. A rabbit can see forward, upward, backward and sideward—but in each of these directions with only one eye. What the world looks like to a rabbit is impossible for humans to imagine because we have binocular vision like cats. Thus it is probable that we see things pretty much as cats do—although they are believed to be color-blind, and also we can never be sure quite *how* they see things because their brains are constructed differently from ours. Nevertheless the general view that we take in is probably similar; less limited than what is seen by dogs, many of which tend to be near-sighted; more limited than what is seen by cats, whose eyesight is considerably sharper than humans'.

Thus, though the eyes in both animals face forward, this characteristic is far more pronounced in the eye-dependent cat than the nose-dependent dog. A cat's eyes are brought right around in front. They sit, wide and unblinking, on each side of the nose, in the same plane, like an owl's. Cats never look out of the corners of their eyes at things. They swivel their heads and stare directly at them. A dog, by contrast, will lie on the floor, its chin outstretched, and if it wants to look at something it will often roll its eyes upward without moving its head at all.

There is a great danger of error in drawing anatomical conclusions from mere appearance. It is tempting to judge the quality of a cat's eye from just looking at it. It is so clear and cold and uncompromising that it *must* be a good optical instrument. In this case the emotional judgment is the correct one. Cat's eyes are splendid instruments. They can apparently focus clearly at any distance, from a few inches to infinity, their power of resolution is high and they are superb accommodaters. One need only observe a cat intently watching a fly as it buzzes about a room to realize how good this accommodation is. The speed and small size of the fly, and its quick changes of position from near to far, all give trouble to humans, but they do not bother a cat. A man will lose sight of the fly repeatedly, and it is only when it shows up against a windowpane or a white wall that he can pick it up again. A cat can keep its eye on any fly with ease—if it can be bothered to do so.

A cat has the largest eye in proportion to its body size of any carnivore. It also has a pupil of great flexibility. In the larger cats it is round, but in smaller cats it narrows to a distinctive vertical slit. All infant cats have blue eyes, but in the adults the color changes to various shades and beautiful mixtures of green, gold and yellow.

The last thing worth noting about the eyes of cats is their efficiency in poor light. Although no animal can see in complete darkness, cats can manage to make things out when it is almost completely dark. The light-sensitive layers at the back of a cat's eye are densely packed with cells, and behind them is a reflecting layer. The light hitting them and triggering off impulses to the brain goes right through these cells, is reflected back and passes through them a second time, sending a second impulse to the brain. In effect, a cat gets double use—coming and going—out of any light that enters its eye. That is why the eyes of cats and other nocturnal animals seem to glow in the dark. They are not actually glowing; they are merely reflecting back at you the light that you are shining at them.

The final special piece of equipment in a cat's head is its tongue. This is covered with small projections called papillae, which resemble the points on a wood rasp. Among house cats the papillae are smaller and give only a slightly rough feeling when one's hand is licked. But among the larger cats the papillae are formidable instruments. A few swipes from a lion's tongue could take the skin right off the back of a human hand. They are an important part of the feeding equipment, and they cut through flesh with surprising speed. A pride of hungry lions around a freshly killed zebra will polish it off in half an hour. All the bones will be licked clean—except those of the lower legs, which have little flesh on them and are often left for jackals and other scavengers.

Cats have a simple way of drinking. A thirsty cat simply lowers its tongue into water and lifts it up into the mouth again. Each papilla acts as a tiny cup and together they hold a surprising amount of liquid. In proportion a cat's tongue is much smaller than a dog's, presumably because it is not used as a cooling device and does not have to be extended as is a dog's tongue when panting. A dog, of course, lacks papillae. It drinks by making a dipper out of the tip of its long slender tongue, curling it under and back, and lifting water into its mouth one slurp at a time. This is a rather sloppy method, and a thirsty dog will scatter water all around its drinking bowl. By contrast a cat is unfailingly dainty. Its tongue moves in and out with great speed and regularity, never spilling a drop.

A cat's body is long and supple. Its bones, though not particularly large for the size of the animal, get their strength from the density of their material. They do not have the porous quality of the bones of many of the larger herbivores. Along with these moderate-sized but strong bones goes a set of equally strong muscles and sinews on which the bones are rather loosely strung together, and it is this loose structure that gives a cat its surpassing grace and sinuosity of movement. No dog can arch its back the way a cat can; no dog has as much freedom in the lateral movement of its legs; nor can a dog sleep curled in as tight a ball, with its head lying on its own shoulder. Such movements are made possible in cats by the arrangement of shoulder blade, collar bone and breast bone. In many animals, including humans, these are attached by powerful ligaments. In cats nothing holds them together except muscles.

All cats' legs (with the exception of the cheetah's, which are unusually long) are moderate in length and again characterized by great strength. Not only do they provide sudden power for springing on prey, but they also serve well in fighting, tipped as they are with the sharpest claws of all carnivores. These claws are under the control of their owner and ordinarily are kept out of sight. A dog has little or no control of its claws. They just sit there, large and rather blunt, on the ends of the toes, growing slowly, and slowly being worn down by friction with the ground as the animal moves around. Anybody who has lived in a New York apartment (particularly one of the newer ones with their paper-thin insulation) will know if the family directly overhead owns a dog by the faint clicking its claws make as it trots about on the hardwood floor. The presence of a cat up there would never be known. Unless it began to yowl, it would be as silent and discreet as a goldfish.

A cat walks on its toes, or more properly with its weight distributed between the toes and the ball of the foot. A normal cat has five toes on the forepaw and four on the hindpaw, although many domestic cats have six or even seven toes on their forepaws. Whether these abnormalities extend to the larger species I do not know. But in the normal paw only four of the toes touch the ground. The fifth—the thumb—exists in the form of a "dewclaw" hanging from the back of the leg just above the ground. The dewclaw has two known uses, and may have others. The cheetah uses it to help seize its prey; the lion to dislodge uncomfortably large pieces of meat that it has attempted to swallow. The hind leg of a cat lacks a dewclaw; it has disappeared through the process of evolution.

A cat's claws do not touch the ground when it walks. They are attached by ligaments to the bone at the tip of each toe and can be extended at will. Retracted, they keep out of the way and do not get blunted. Among the smaller cats they are almost as sharp as needles, and even among the lion and tiger they come to remarkably fine points. Backed by its powerful leg muscles, a lion's claws are awesome weapons. Three or four convulsive kicks, delivered at blinding speed and with full force, can disembowel a horse. It is this combination of sharp tooth and powerful jaw linked with equally sharp claw and powerful leg muscle that makes such a formidable animal out of a cat. Size for size, it can beat its weight in anything but other cats. And with claws like that, a cat can afford to give up a little something in the way of a jaw. A wolf, by contrast, must do all of its killing and all its fighting with its teeth; it is not surprising that its jaw is larger and more versatile than a cat's.

In overall body proportions the cats are remarkably alike, although there are a few obvious variations. The cheetah is atypical in seeming to have legs that are too long and a head that is too small. The male lion seems to have too large a head, the serval too large ears. Otherwise all cats fit the cattish mold to a nicety. All have long tails except the lynxes and a few domestic varieties like the Manx cat. Where the lynx and Manx tails went—and why—no one knows, for tails are certainly among the most expressive of a cat's appurtenances. They curl and coil snugly in sleep. They loop and droop in ineffable indolence from leopards drowsing in trees. They switch back and forth with hair-raising tension in a cat about to spring. They stand straight as masts in a confident kitchen-strolling tabby. And their tips are capable of the minutest nuances of expression, tilting daintily one way or another for only an inch at the end. One species, the lion, has a large tuft of hair at the tip of its tail, and this conceals a sharp spur, or nail, whose purpose is unknown. It was once believed that the lion used it to lash itself into a proper lionlike rage, but this idea has long since been exploded—though, as the African wildlife expert Armand Denis points out, "we have nothing better to put in its place."

The coats of cats vary in color, although the great majority of them tend to be tawny in tone—presumably for concealment. Spots, polka dots, rosettes and stripes abound. Even lions, which appear to be a uniform sandy hue, are spotted when young, and many of them carry faint spots on their flanks and legs well up into maturity. Every once in a while there is a furor in East Africa over the discovery of a new species of spotted lion. But each new species—so far—has always dwindled to a few isolated individuals whose spots are more persistent than the norm. Considering the wide prevalence of spots and stripes in adult cats, and their universality among the young of all species, it is probable that the early ancestors of cats were also distinctly marked. But whether they were predominantly spotted or predominantly striped, there is no way of knowing. This is one of the frustrating aspects of the study of extinct animals. Though scientists can put their skeletons together, reconstruct their shapes from the most sophisticated conjectures about the size and location of muscles and go on from there to build up the tissues that covered them, they simply do not know the color of any extinct animal except one or two, like the woolly mammoth, specimens of which have been miraculously preserved for thousands of years in ice. Red-white-and-blue dinosaurs? Perhaps; there are even wilder-colored lizards still walking the earth.

About the only thing that seems a certainty in the markings of the long-gone ancestral cats is the tear stripe, a dark mark running from the inner corner of each eye. Every living species of cat, in whatever continent, has this distinctive eye mark, also some pattern of stripes or spots running upward from the eyes toward the crown.

The coat, or fur, that bears all these markings also varies. As a general rule, the larger the species the coarser the hairs. Thus, a lion cannot properly be considered to have fur at all since fur, by definition, must be soft, fine and thick. A lion's hairs are for the most part coarse and tend to be all of a size. They are also short, as befits an animal living in a hot climate. They lie flat against the skin, somewhat in the manner of the coat of a cow or horse, and nothing at all like the delicious deep coats of some of the little cats, with their inner fur of a softness not to be believed. Fine or coarse, the coat grows in a skin that is hung so loosely on the cat's body that it might almost seem to have been designed for an animal one size larger. This loose skin is a great asset in fighting, for it can stand a great deal of pulling and tearing without damage to the tissues and organs that it covers.

This, then, is the architecture of cats. Considering their great differences in size (it takes about 30 average male house cats to equal the weight of one fully grown male lion), their distribution over all the continents except Australia and Antarctica, and their adjustment to a wide variety of habitats —ranging from the snow-covered slopes and birch groves of the Himalayas to the sopping rain forests of Central America and the near-desert conditions

of parts of Equatorial Africa—cats are astonishingly alike. And it must be repeated that the reason for this similarity is that they are the nearest thing
to a perfect stalking, hunting animal that the evolutionary process has yet
produced. How and when modern cats first appeared is not known exactly.
The family trees of many types of animals are full of irritating gaps, and
the branch that leads to cats from the primitive miacid carnivores is one
such. There are distressingly few catlike fossils lying about. Paleontologists
have speculated that others may turn up in Asia (where all cats are believed to have radiated from) when more intensive digging and sifting of fos-
sil-bearing strata is undertaken there. There are huge areas in Western
China, Mongolia, Siberia, Burma, Assam and the various Himalayan states
where no paleontologist has yet set foot.

Despite the scarcity of fossils, this much *is* known. Cats of sufficient mo-
dernity to share the family Latin name of *Felidae* with today's species
were certainly on the scene five million years ago, and may have been in existence as much as 10 million years ago. But even at that remote date there
were already two distinct types, as the chart opposite makes clear. One
group includes the ancestors of the quick lithe cats of today. The other includes a somewhat heavier, presumably slower and more powerful type
adapted to prey on the large and slow herbivores of the time. This branch
of the family is epitomized by one of the most famous and puzzling fossil
creatures known to man, the Ice-Age saber-tooth "tiger," or *Smilodon*.

The puzzle of the saber-tooth began with the first discovery of its fossils, and centered on the enormous fangs that the upper canines of this
animal had developed into. In the largest saber-tooths these fangs exceeded
eight inches in length—a pair of curved daggers extending down from the
upper jaw and, when the mouth was closed, even some distance below the
bottom of the lower jaw. The belief is that they were enclosed by a large
droopy lip that also hung down from the lower jaw. The question that was
first asked about the saber-tooth was: how did it get its jaw open wide
enough to eat? I remember hearing about this extraordinary animal as a
boy in school and being told by my biology teacher that it was extinct because its teeth had grown too large to be manageable and it had starved
to death. This, of course, was ridiculous, for saber-tooths of various kinds
managed to get along with, and undoubtedly depended on, those oversized
fangs for a period of nearly 40 million years. In fact, so successful was this
adaptation that it appeared more than once during the history of the cats, as
the chart also shows.

So the puzzle about the saber-tooth is not how it managed despite its

The chart opposite shows in simplified
form one of the latest theories about cat
evolution and suggests a fascinating
possibility: that the cats have followed
the same evolutionary course not once but
twice. About 40 million years ago certain
miacid descendants had already begun to
develop catlike traits. These were the
Paleofelids (*at lower right of chart*). One
group, the Nimravines, was slender and
quick like modern cats. The other was
heavier, slower and stronger, and gradually
developed the great stabbing teeth that
marked them as saber-tooths. Both lines
were successful for nearly 30 million years
and then became extinct for unknown
reasons.

Meanwhile the main cat line of Neofelids
was also evolving, and about 20 million
years ago had produced *Pseudaelurus,*
whose descendants quite independently
repeated the history of the extinct
Paleofelids. For the second time, a line of
heavy husky saber-tooths appeared,
culminating in *Smilodon*, the largest and
last of its kind. At the same time the
quicker smaller cats continued their own
independent development and eventually
became the cats of today (*top of chart*).
However, for a long time none of them
were very large. The only "big cats" for a
period of about five million years were a
group of rather primitive animals like
Dinofelis (*at left of chart*). They were
the size of today's lions, and disappeared
at about the time modern lions and tigers
came on the scene.

THE EVOLUTION OF THE CATS

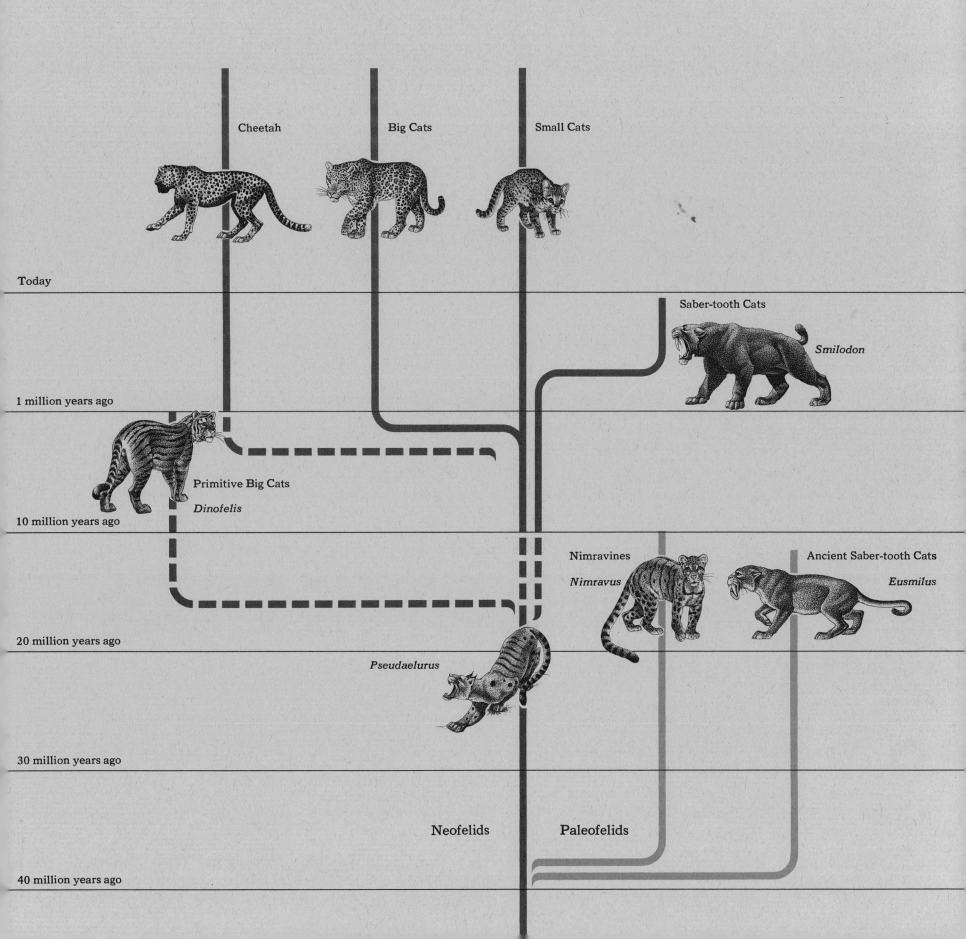

Cheetah

Big Cats

Small Cats

Saber-tooth Cats

Smilodon

Today

1 million years ago

Primitive Big Cats

Dinofelis

10 million years ago

Nimravines

Nimravus

Ancient Saber-tooth Cats

Eusmilus

20 million years ago

Pseudaelurus

30 million years ago

Neofelids

Paleofelids

40 million years ago

large fangs, but how it used them. It is almost universally agreed today that they were employed as stabbing weapons. Several saber-tooths, the *Smilodon* of North America in particular, had enormously powerful necks and neck muscles, and the belief is that they did their prey to death with lethal downward thrusts of their giant canines. Other factors support this idea. For one thing, the lower jaw of the saber-tooth was relatively weak and its ability to bite and tear somewhat limited. For another, the whole animal was large and heavily built, as if to give it the weight and leverage necessary to make such an attack. The biggest saber-tooths were bigger than modern tigers and a great deal heavier. Furthermore, there was an abundance of large prey animals in existence during their heyday, of just the kind that a husky saber-tooth might be able to handle. Many of these, like the young of mammoths, mastodons and giant ground sloths, were large, slow, stolid animals weighing a ton or more. Like the saber-tooths, they are now all extinct, and it is reasonable to suppose that the predator followed its prey into oblivion.

The last of the saber-tooths disappeared about 10 thousand years ago, and since there were plenty of other herbivores around—many of which have survived into modern times—a natural question arises: why did not the saber-tooths switch to them? The answer must be that they were not equipped to do so. They were presumably too slow or too clumsy to make a living on the alert and swift zebras, the wild horses and larger antelopes that had evolved by that time and still populate the grasslands of the earth. What is the use of a magnificent set of ivory stabbers backed up by the biggest neck muscles in the family if there is nothing around big enough and slow enough to stab?

What did survive is the less specialized branch of the cat family. Its members descend from an extinct ancestor called *Pseudaelurus*, which put in an appearance in Eurasia about 20 million years ago. *Pseudaelurus* was fairly small, about the size of a lynx or bobcat. It cannot have cut much of a figure alongside the more dramatic saber-tooth, but it was quick and strong for its size; and with equipment almost identical with that of modern cats, it could live on smaller, quicker things that a saber-tooth could not catch. Gradually it made its way into a number of niches, undergoing various specializations as it did so. The end product is about three dozen species of cats that inhabit the earth today. Of these, eleven are found in Africa. It is with them that the rest of this book will concern itself.

THE LION

Today there is a better chance of observing African lions in their natural state than at any time in a century or more. This golden opportunity cannot last. Twenty years from now it probably will have changed for the worse. In a hundred years, when the swelling tide of humanity has swept over Africa, it may be gone. But right now, in East and South Africa, in the big game reserves, the lions are on perfect display. Getting to know them is easy, and for the patient observer it is a wonderful experience.

That this moment *is* an opportunity needs some explanation and requires a look back to a time some thousands of years ago when human beings were a negligible influence in the ecology of Africa. The land was endless, its carrying capacity of animals immense. The biggest species— elephant and rhinoceros—occupied it like living fortresses, secure within their own size and might. As long as they remained healthy nothing could touch them. They came and went, generation after generation, preoccupied with their own affairs, untroubled most of the time by any predator, affected only by the larger caprices of drought, flood and pestilence. Nobody knows how many rhinos there were in Africa before men developed the capacity and the inclination to bother them, but estimates run up into the millions. The herds of antelope and other grazers and browsers were far larger. Like tides of flesh, they drifted across the savanna, and the lions lived on them.

Lions were everywhere except in the deserts and rain forests. Reliable estimates of their total numbers are almost impossible to arrive at today. Not only are we ignorant of how many lions-per-square-mile of land there were (since this varied constantly with the density of game animals), but we do not even know how many square miles of suitable land there were (since this also varied as a result of droughts and other climatological changes). Still, Africa was so huge that local variability probably evened itself out over the entire continent to provide an average figure—if not for any given year or decade, certainly over a century or more. The only way to start in making an estimate of this sort is to note the relationship between lions and game today. This has been measured in game parks and other places—with the number running all the way from 10 to 40 lions-per-hundred-square-miles in well-stocked game country. Now, looking at the continent as a whole, and taking another wild stab at how much of it—on the average—might have been suitable for game, we come up with a figure of five million square miles. Thus, for some thousands of years—ever since the stabilization of the present African climate after the last Ice Age—it is probable that there were at least a half million lions in Africa, and there may have been as many as two million.

During that entire time, of course, there were men living in Africa, but for most of it they were little or no trouble to the lions. The men were few, and originally they were pastoralists, preoccupied with their herds. They had no basic interest in either game or lions. Later, when settled agricultural societies slowly developed in Africa, the farmers and the game herds tended increasingly to separate. The former worked their gardens, the latter stayed out in the open savanna, and the lions stayed with them. Still, it is certain that every village boy who ever grew up in lion country saw lions from time to time and learned how to protect himself, his family and his stock from their occasional depredations. Equally certain is that every village had its long toll of people killed by lions and its legends of brave men who had succeeded in killing lions in reprisal.

For the pastoralists, the situation was somewhat different. They wandered over the grassland, sharing this environment with the wild game, and as a result they came into contact with lions constantly. Wherever people and cattle became numerous enough to attract the attention of lions, the people had to learn to deal with them, for cows are easier to kill than zebras. The life led by the Masai today is a perfect example of this kind of pastoralism. To survive, they have had to make it their business to contend with lions, and they do so very well. They build temporary habitations called manyattas, clusters of mud and dung huts that they surround with high, dense thorn hedges so that their cattle can be corralled inside at night. During the day they take their herds out to graze, watching over them carefully as they do so. All Masai men are initiated into manhood between the ages of 16 and 20, and become warriors, privileged to go on hunting and raiding expeditions, and to carry long sharp spears wherever they go. A Masai is never separated from his spear, and part of his philosophy of life is to prove his bravery as a man among men. He does this,

in company with a small band of friends, by tracking down lions and killing them—with only a hide shield to protect him and only his spear as a
weapon. Daring is the thing, and the man who gains the most credit is the
one who first succeeds in darting in and seizing the lion by the tail. The
Masai have a healthy respect for lions but they are not afraid of them. If
anything, the shoe is on the other foot. In Masai country lions avoid humans, recognizing them as the only dangerous enemies they have.

This was the situation in tribal Africa for centuries—an uneasy standoff
between man and lion—until the modern invasion of the continent by European settlers, first in North and South Africa, later in East Africa,
eventually everywhere. With the introduction of firearms, concentrated
slaughter of game and predators was possible, and both were systematically
eliminated from the land as nuisances to large-scale farming and stock raising. The speed and ruthlessness of this extermination is beyond belief. Up
until about 1896 herds of springbok numbering in the millions were frequently seen in the Cape Province of South Africa. Forty years later those
herds had vanished. Similar stories involving other creatures followed
through the years, and the process can be traced all the way down to a pitifully small but telling anecdote dating from as recently as 1962. A white
Kenya farmer was complaining to a visiting American about a herd of 40 zebras that bothered him by grazing on land he wished to be kept for the exclusive use of his cows.

"How did you keep them off?" he was asked.

"I shot them," he said unconcernedly. "Every last bloody one."

"Are there any lions around here now?"

"One or two, I imagine. Though I haven't seen one in quite a bit."

"What will they eat, now that the zebras are gone?"

"Dunno. But if I see any I'll blast them too. They can be devils with cattle, you know."

When wild animals interfere with human interests they are quickly exterminated. A species like the lion gets it from two directions. The animals
that he normally lives on become scarcer. At the same time he is himself
hunted because he is a menace to cattle and to human beings. At what
point the lion population of Africa hit bottom is impossible to determine,
but it was probably some time between 1920 and 1950. Many factors
enter here and they are not likely ever to be sorted out. Hunting safaris
took an increasing toll, particularly after the introduction of the automobile,
which suddenly opened up remote country accessible in the past only to
wealthy sportsmen who could afford elaborate expeditions requiring months

of time and scores of native porters. Less obvious, but far more important in the long run, was a steady acceleration in the settlement of the land by both Africans and whites during the first half of the 20th Century. European police control put an end to tribal warfare; European medicine and hygienic practices lowered the native death rate; European efforts to eliminate the tsetse fly opened up large areas that hitherto had been denied to humans because of the lethal diseases that the fly gave both to man and his cattle. These three factors have produced a population rise whose rate in certain parts of Africa is as high as any in the world. In Kenya it is compounding itself at an annual rate of nearly three per cent, which does not sound like much, but which will result in a doubling of the population every 25 years.

With this surge of humanity the pressures to occupy more and more land became increasingly severe. The game became more and more hard-pressed. And lions began to become almost invisible, having learned the hard way that man was a more powerful force than they. From being the confident proprietors of their domain, abroad at whatever hour of the day or night that suited them, they had become nocturnal. In some places they even stopped their celebrated nightly roaring, and took to communicating with each other only by subdued and cautious grunts.

This is not to say that they were never encountered, or that when they were, they were any less dangerous than before; only that they were far less numerous, and infinitely more cautious in their behavior toward humans. As a result, the visitor to Africa, whether as a hunter or a mere observer of wild life, could not be sure of seeing any lions at all, much less getting close enough to study them in any detail.

What changed this was the establishment of national game parks and reserves, first in South Africa, later in the Congo and East Africa. In Kenya and Tanzania alone over 52 thousand square miles of land have been set aside for game since 1940. There was some fear, in the general turmoil incident to the establishment of these countries as independent states, that the game parks might not survive. On the contrary, the new governments regard the parks and their populations of animals as extraordinary national assets. They are determined to preserve them, partly from a justifiable national pride, partly from the recognition that they will become a unique tourist attraction in the years to come.

The animals within the parks have responded nobly. Aside from occasional "cropping" to reduce populations that become too large and threaten to do permanent damage to the vegetation, the animals live in a state of complete natural balance. The lions have reverted to their former relaxed and careless ways, and in places like the Mara National Reserve or the Serengeti National Park they may be found without difficulty almost any day in the year.

One's first encounter with a pride of lions in such a setting is an unforgettable experience. It is a late afternoon in the Mara Reserve. The weight of the equatorial sun has begun to lift. The air is clear and golden. The Land Rover bounces gently across the plain. Irregular clumps of wildebeest, zebra and gazelle extend to the horizon, their outlines brought to an unbelievable sharpness in the low level light. Suddenly someone says: "lions!"

It is as simple as that. There they are, 15 of them, a couple of fine males, half a dozen females and an assortment of cubs—all lying in a stupor, scattered over the ground like tawny bolsters, drunk with sleep, sun and food. They lie sprawled in every conceivable attitude, like dead soldiers on a battlefield, and they might as well be dead for all the attention they pay to the approaching Land Rover. Long familiarity with those noisy, smelly machines in the game reserves has taught lions that they are neither edible nor dangerous, and their attitude toward them goes far beyond contempt—it approaches utter indifference.

The Land Rover stops 20 feet away. The man standing in the roof-hatch busies himself with his camera. One shaggy head may rise up. There will be a momentary glitter of a brilliant amber eye, a prodigious yawn that gives a glimpse of two fearsome canines and a foot or so of pink throat, and the head will fall again with an audible thump on the ground. The other members of the pride will not stir. And even the yawner will somehow have managed to get across the idea that the vehicle's approach had nothing to do with him. He was going to yawn anyway.

Thus, the lion, once again a king in his own country, relaxed to a degree of regal languor incomprehensible to humans—interested in other lions, in eating when he gets hungry, in nothing else.

The watchers settle down to wait. For a while nothing happens beyond a yawn or two. Then two small cubs wake up and begin to explore the nipples of a lioness who is stretched on her back, one paw stuck straight up in the air. Nothing doing there—the well is dry. But the female gives a grunt and rolls over on her side. Her tail twitches and instantly the cubs attack it. The next five minutes are given over to an enchanting display of baby-lion fun, ambushes and pounces, miniature growls, collapses on rubber legs. An infant lion seems all head and ears, a comically big head, an enormous furry triangle of a head with a nose to match, a head so large as to overbalance the body behind it. With a head like that, who could stand up or run properly? These cubs do neither. They plunge and stagger drunkenly, all the time wearing expressions of blue-eyed solemnity on their gigantic faces that are excruciatingly funny. Small lion cubs are among the most irresistible of all young animals.

So beguiling have been the activities of the two cubs that the watchers in the car have not been paying attention to the other members of the pride. Suddenly it is clear that they are coming to. They do this gradually, to the tune of a great deal of stretching and luxurious rolling. A couple of lean and handsome lionesses sit up and stare off into space. The old man shakes himself and looks glassily around. There is a certain amount of socializing. Heads are butted affectionately, licks are exchanged, eyes brighten. Within an hour there has been a complete transformation from lethargy to a quite remarkable alertness. The lions are wide awake now, and they are getting hungry. Several of the older animals begin looking intently in one direction. Others look expectantly at them. Then a large lioness gets up and walks in the direction of the Land Rover.

Some recognition at last? Not at all: the car could be a tree stump or a boulder for all the attention she pays it. Looking straight ahead, she passes within three feet of it, and those inside could put out their hands and touch her if they felt so inclined. Instead they watch the play of her shoulders under her tawny skin, looking almost directly down on her as she strides purposefully by. Another lioness follows, and another. The little cubs are now sitting up all in a row, watching the departure of their elders with intense interest. They know—everybody knows—that the business of the evening is about to start.

The lion's Latin name is *Leo leo*. It once was *Felis leo* (cat-lion), placing it, systematically speaking, in one genus with other cats. Every cat in the world was once a *Felis* in the eyes of science, but no longer. Recent classification has grouped certain larger members of the family (the lion, tiger, jaguar, leopard and snow leopard) into the genus of *Leo*, leaving the rest of the cats in the genus *Felis*. One species, the cheetah *(Acinonyx jubatus)*, is left out of this classification. As will be seen, that animal belongs by itself, having special characteristics that fit it neither with its larger cousins nor its smaller ones.

There are those who believe that the lion also deserves a special pigeon hole to itself, in recognition of three characteristics that set it apart. First is the already-mentioned tail claw, that peculiar sharp nail hidden in the tuft of hair at the tip of the tail. Second is the mane, a shaggy ruff that covers the top of the head, the throat, neck and sometimes the shoulders and upper chest. This varies in size and color from lion to lion, but it is always present in some degree among males. It is the first and most prominent feature that distinguishes male from female lions. Slight sexual dimorphism—differences in size and appearance between males and females—is fairly common among cats. The female is apt to be smaller and more slightly built, but otherwise they tend to resemble each other so closely that in the field it is usually difficult, if not impossible, to tell them apart. Not so among lions. Thanks principally to its mane, but also to its more massive build, its larger head and deeper chest, a fully grown male is so different from a female that it can be identified instantly—often at a considerable distance. The third peculiarity of the lion is its gregariousness. Where other cats live alone or in pairs, lions are extremely sociable and are usually found in family groups, or prides, that may contain 20 or more individuals.

A pride is a loose grouping and seems to follow no set rule. Its basic unit is the family, a mother and her cubs. But as these grow up and are followed by new sets of babies, the teenagers and young adults may stay together, and the pride will slowly grow. Or two or three females with their cubs (or without them) may join together to form a pride. There is obviously an advantage in numbers in the kind of cooperative hunting that lions do, and it is perhaps for that reason, as much as for their extremely sociable natures, that lions tend to remain in groups.

There is a definite hierarchy within the pride. The largest and strongest male—or at least the one that succeeds in convincing the other males of his superiority—is at the top. He is followed in order by the other fully grown males if any, then by the females in the order of their strength and seniority, finally by the adolescents. Small cubs come under the protection of their own mothers. Lion society is a curious mixture of easy-going relaxation of these rules and ferocious observance of them. Relationships seem so amiable and affectionate most of the time that when enforcement is in order, it often comes with shocking suddenness. The two things that interest lions are food and sex, and if the number-one male is deterred in any way from the speedy realization of his goal in either of these departments, there is an instant and occasionally fatal retaliation.

Prides vary in the tightness of their organization. This depends in some measure on the living conditions. In open savanna areas where the game tends to move seasonally and where hunting may require some cooperation, the prides tend to hang together. And if there is plenty of game, they may grow very large. Groups of 20 or more are not uncommon, and a record sighting of 35 was once made in Kruger National Park. Of course, if the game becomes scarce these large groups cannot survive together, and they break up again into smaller units. In scrub or bush country where the herbivore population may be more constant and the terrain more broken up, the lion population in a particular area may join and separate with greater fluidity. But everywhere there will be a certain amount of coming and going— mothers departing to bear cubs in solitude, young adult males drifting off, or more often being driven off by the dominant male, to form bachelor prides of their own. There are also old males who have been kicked out of the pride by younger, stronger rivals, and who end their days morosely, living alone. Often the dominant lion will simply decide not to live with the pride, but will set up bachelor quarters with a male friend. Close bonds of affection are often developed between males who, like a couple of clubmen, prefer their own to mixed company. In this way they are spared the bickerings of females and the teasing of cubs, but they stay close enough to keep an eye on what is going on, making sure to show up regularly for meals and sex. They may not spend their days with the pride, but they are still the bosses, and all concerned know it.

The teaming up of a pair of strong males also assures control of the pride. No single lion, no matter how experienced or powerful, could stand up against two healthy and determined adversaries; and one of the ways in which the head of a pride may be dislodged is by a pair of young friends who, singly, could not have mustered the courage or the skills to drive him off. The problems facing such partnerships often come *after* the dethronement has taken place. Lion society, in common with any other communal animal society, is based directly on force or on the threat of it. ''The lion's share'' is no throw-away phrase; it has real and terrible meaning, deriving from the belief held by all lions that the shortest distance between desire and its realization is a straight line. You want something— you go directly for it. The only thing that can stop you is something larger or more dangerous than you. Thus, though a couple of young lions in the first flush of full lionhood may collaborate successfully to gain control of a pride (or a territory containing females) the collaboration may be a short one.

Charles A.W. Guggisberg, the author of *Simba*, the best book ever written on lions, kept one such bachelor pair under observation for several years in Nairobi National Park. This partnership was remarkable in that it was so durable. Guggisberg christened this pair Hildebrand and Hadubrand, after two legendary heroes from an ancient Germanic epic. The human Hildebrand was a great fighter who went off to war, leaving an infant son behind him. Years later on his way homeward he was forced to face a challenge by a magnificent young warrior who stood in his way. It was only when they got down to the business of chopping each other into pieces that Hildebrand realized that his adversary was his own son Hadubrand. He tried to explain this to Hadubrand, even offered him some presents, but the younger man merely sneered at him for trying to find a coward's way out of a fight he was going to lose. Unfortunately the manuscript in which this tale is preserved is a fragment. It is broken off at this point, and we never do find out whether or not Hildebrand managed to make his story stick before his head was separated from his body.

Nevertheless, Guggisberg's choice of these names was a singularly appropriate one. The lion Hildebrand was the older, and originally the more feisty, of the two. He got his way most of the time, apparently because Hadubrand had an amiable temper for a lion and was willing to have it so. This may well have been nothing more than habit—the two may have joined forces at a time when Hadubrand had yet to gain his full strength and was not prepared to assert his full authority. How they originally got together Guggisberg does not know. They suddenly appeared in the Nairobi Park, a husky pair of buccaneers, ready for anything. They chased off the reigning monarch and promptly took control of an area of about 55 square miles. A number of lionesses lived within their domain, some singly, some in small, shifting groups. Hildebrand and Hadubrand had their way with them at will, driving away other hopeful suitors as fast as they appeared. Their only mutual disagreements arose from disputes over sex, and for a while Hildebrand won these; Guggisberg remembers seeing Hadubrand on one occasion with a badly clawed nose. But in addition to being short-tempered and strong-willed, Hildebrand was apparently a sensible lion. As he grew older he began to realize that he was no longer a match for his partner, and he discreetly threw his weight around less and less. Hadubrand became the boss—but they remained friends. A curious consequence of this shift in authority was that, as a team, they lost some control of their territory. Hildebrand was no longer energetic enough to carry his share of patrolling it, and Hadubrand could not carry the load by himself. As a result, other lions moved into the edges and succeeded in mating with lionesses that the partners formerly would have managed to keep for themselves—that is, mostly for Hildebrand.

In considering lion territories, it should be borne in mind that these are not rigidly determined. For males, the territorial determinant seems to be mainly sexual; they consider certain females to be theirs, and wherever those females make a habit of being, that is where the lion's boundaries are. Like many other animals, lions urinate on bushes to mark their claims, but they do not patrol their own property, nor inspect others', with anything like the compulsiveness that some species such as wolves display.

For the female lion, territoriality is principally a matter of sustenance; she needs a hunting area of a certain size, or at least of a certain productivity. Obviously a hunting area where game is scarce must be larger than one where game is plentiful. And in places where the game migrates there can be no territories at all in the narrow sense of the word, because the hunters simply travel with their prey, sometimes covering hundreds of miles in a single season.

But, be they stay-at-homes or wanderers, lions are gregarious. Except for an occasional wretched, lonely old male, they live their lives together—lives that are more complex and also more hazardous than would appear to the lion student who first comes across a pride sprawled out and sleeping off a big meal in the African sun.

The cycle of lion existence begins when a female comes into heat. This first occurs when she is about three years old, and continues at three-week intervals through the year unless she is pregnant. Her span of fertility is believed to cover about seven years or a little more, after which she is an old lady. The period of estrus itself lasts about five days. Her urine develops a strong, characteristic smell, as does a discharge from the anal gland, and these attract any males in the vicinity like wasps to honey. In a normal pride there is no question as to who will have the privilege of mating with a newly receptive female; it will be the top male. Others get their chance only when two or more females come into heat at the same time. But if there is only one, and if the top male is not sated from another just-finished affair, he will quickly dispose of any ambitious youngsters who may wish to dispute his claim.

It is only when a powerful younger member of the pride (or a stranger wandering in) decides that he is strong enough to challenge the leader that a real fight develops. Sexual battles can be ferocious in the extreme, and sometimes go to the death. One safari party heard such a fight going on for four hours during the night. The next morning the campers followed a trail of torn and ripped-up grass spattered with blood and bits of hair for three miles. At the end was a very large lion dead of a broken neck, his entire body gashed with dreadful bites. Obviously it had been an even struggle, and a bitterly fought one, for a long time, and the victim must have thought—right up to the end—that he had a chance of winning or he would have broken off and run away.

In most cases, however, nothing so dramatic happens. A growl or two from the old man, and the female is his. From that moment he is extremely attentive to her. Sometimes their courtship takes place in company with other members of the pride, but more often the mated couple goes off by itself. The lazy, sleepy demeanor of the male vanishes. He is all attention. If his partner gets up, so does he. If she walks about, he is right there, his head a few inches from the base of her tail. When she lies down he flops down beside her. Intermittently he will copulate with her. The sexual vigor of a healthy lion in the bloom of life is remarkable. He will mate every 20 or 30 minutes for hours at a time. There is a report of a caged pair in the Dresden Zoo that mated 360 times during an eight-day period. But this must not be regarded as typical because the captivity of the animals may have intensified their preoccupation with sexual matters. It is known that young captive males are more precocious than wild ones.

Lion courtship has little of the fierceness commonly found among other cats. For many of the smaller species a certain amount of clawing and biting is part of the act, and the male may set his teeth in the neck of his partner during copulation. The reason for this behavior pattern is not well understood, although it may be that it is the cat's way of ensuring that she is mated with a strong and able partner. If she puts up a certain amount of resistance, it will take a powerful and determined male to claw and bite her into submission. A feeble or unaggressive male will be unable to do so, and therefore will not perpetuate his undesirable traits. It is one of the marvels of evolution that such patterns of behavior emerge, for they have as much to do with the shaping and survival of species as do physical characteristics. In fact they are, in a very large sense, the instruments by which physical characteristics are developed. For among higher animals it is sexual choice between partners that determines which characteristics will be preserved and intensified. And, of course, it is the development of certain genetic habit patterns that decides the direction in which those choices will go.

What is equally remarkable about the process is that it is self-regulating. It is just as well that lions do not engage in such rough sexual activity; they are so immensely strong that sexual fighting during mating for the improvement of the breed could defeat its own purpose by causing serious, perhaps fatal, injury to the breeders. "How neat," we say, or "how lucky that lions don't happen to have those awful traits." But it is not a question of either neatness or luck. It is simply the law of natural selection working in its relentlessly logical way. Lions which persist in acting brutally during mating cannot perpetuate their brutal natures because that very brutality will kill their mates more often than not. As a result, more gentle lions will in the long run produce many more offspring than the brutal ones, and, to the extent that they do, the species as a whole will evolve toward a pattern of nonviolent mating. But lions are still cats and the ancestral habits still lurk among their genetic shadows. Certain males are rough, and there are records of lionesses that have actually been bitten to death while in the act of mating.

Among the species as evolved today, however, the vast majority of mated pairs are conspicuously affectionate. The females are often frankly seductive, lolling against their mates, rolling and stretching luxuriously. The male, for his part, if not bothered by the presence of possible rivals hanging about, often looks foolishly bemused and lovelorn. He is obviously totally absorbed by his mate. Physical closeness is important. He will lie next to her, lick her tenderly. When he decides to copulate he straddles her from behind. The act is performed vigorously and quickly, and on the whole quietly. Sometimes the female will utter a few soft growls, sometimes the male will. Opinion is divided as to whether the male ever roars at this time, many authorities believing that he never does. Of the two mating lions that I have observed, one performed silently, the other did not. This second animal, a splendid specimen in the Ngorongoro Crater, copulated three times while I watched him. Each time, at the end of his act, he gave a short but loud and wrenching grunt. Having so expressed himself, he lay down by his mate again, looking, if lions can be said to do so, highly pleased with himself.

After about a week of intimacy, as the female's estrus ends, so does the romance. Either party, or both, may then rejoin the pride, but they will pay no special attention to each other thereafter. Three and a half months later the lioness will have her cubs. Just before her time comes she will leave the pride and find a secluded place in deep brush or hidden away in some rocks. She will try to select a spot near water and, if possible, one surrounded by thick bushes or tall grass.

Lion litters vary in size, depending on the age of the mother and on the abundance of game. In lean years litters are small, and in a very lean one there may be no litter at all. In any case, for her first family a young lioness will produce one or at most two cubs. During her most fruitful years, usually from age five to age 10, she will have three or four at a time; then, as she grows older, she will begin to taper off again. Because of the helplessness of small cubs and the long time that their mother must devote to them before she can afford to begin thinking of other matters, lionesses give birth only every other year. Thus, if she lives out her allotted span, a lioness will produce, at most, only about 15 cubs during her lifetime, and may produce as few as 10. Of these, only about half will reach maturity.

Only about half . . .? That seems an astonishingly small percentage for so doughty an animal as the lion. Look at that healthy pride described a few pages back sprawled in the Mara Reserve; what on earth could endanger those plump, tumbling cubs, with their watchful mothers and aunts, and those two statuesque males—the fiery embodiment of strength, and radiating a seemingly limitless potential for protection?

Many things can happen to lions. Their lives are not nearly so easy as they might seem, and the troubles begin at birth. One of the things a young lioness must learn is how to be a good mother. Some of them are not. Like teen-age girls, they may be flighty and careless, with undependable maternal instincts. Her first cub may not generate any feelings of responsibility in a young lioness at all. She may abandon it; she may even eat it. Even if she does not, there are a great many things she must learn about hiding, feeding, protecting and teaching before she can begin to give her babies a good chance to grow up. To start with, there is the problem of other lions. No matter how benign and sleepy those big males may look, an implacable ferocity is there just below the surface, and the youngster must learn to respect it, particularly at mealtimes, or his life may be ended abruptly by a single snarling crunch.

All too often a cub may simply starve to death. If his mother is injured and cannot provide for him, he will not survive unless he finds another wet nurse or is old enough to tag along and make his way in the pride on his own. This is often difficult. Later he must go through a trying period of adolescence during which he is susceptible to certain respiratory ailments of a flulike nature. These come along at just the time he may be thrown on his own to hunt and kill for himself—before he has really learned how. Finally, there are accidents, and these are not confined to cubs. Hunting is a violent business, and the hunter is sometimes gored by his prey, or has his leg broken or his paw hopelessly mashed. He may be attacked by a crocodile while drinking at a river, or even trampled in an injudicious argument with an adult elephant—the only African animal that lions ordinarily stay away from. One large lion was sighted by a hunter in a puzzlingly emaciated condition in a country rich with game. When shot, the lion was found to have gotten a piece of wood wedged between his upper teeth and his palate; he was slowly starving to death.

Considering the size they will attain as adults, newborn lions are tiny. A human infant averages about seven pounds at birth, and will grow to be a 170-pound adult—a multiplier of about 25. By contrast, a lion weighs about two pounds at birth and will multiply that weight 200 times at maturity. Newborn lions are about 12 inches long. At first they seem to be all head and paws. Their tails are short and stumpy and have no tufts at their ends. Their coats are almost always spotted, usually heavily so; these spots will gradually fade out during adolescence, more quickly among males than among females. The latter may carry faint spots on their flanks up into middle age. The coat of a baby lion is thick and woolly. It has none of the softness or silkiness of a puppy's or a kitten's but has a somewhat ruglike consistency.

A newborn cub's eyes are a beautiful smoky blue. They have something of the staring innocence of a kitten's, but even more pronounced because of their much larger size. Lion cubs look solemn. At two months the blue in the eye begins to change, and by three months it will have assumed the golden amber hue of adulthood. Many cubs are born with their eyes open; if not, they open up within a day or so. The youngsters are helpless at first. They sleep a great deal of the time, and do little moving except to get at their mother's teats. The lioness has only four teats, and consequently if the litter should contain five cubs, or even six, as has been reported, the cubs usually will have a thin time and some may starve. When the mother is absent, which may be a great deal of the time when game is scarce, the cubs keep very still. This must be deeply ingrained in them because a harried mother may be away for a day or two before she finds food for herself, and the little ones must become extremely hungry and restless during such long absences. Nevertheless, they lie low, and usually they manage to avoid detection by hyenas, their principal enemy. The importance of thick grass or bushes around the den is obvious at this critical time in the lives of the youngsters. A prowling hyena may scent cubs in the thicket, but being unable to see clearly just where they are, it may hesitate to investigate for fear that the lioness may be there too.

When they are about four weeks old the cubs are big enough to begin staggering about and playing with each other. They are now getting ready to leave their hideout, and soon, as they grow in strength, they will begin following their mother. This was the stage that had barely been reached by the youngest family of lions that I have ever seen. They were at most five weeks old when my wife and I came on them near Seronera Lodge in the Serengeti Plain in 1962. The mother was lying in the grass at the edge of a track with four babies around her. We stopped our Land Rover about 30 feet away, and three of the cubs, fearless and full of curiosity, immediately began walking toward us, two of them actually disappearing under the car while I was trying to photograph them. They uttered mewing noises, exactly like kittens but louder.

The mother was more nervous than her young. Seeing them go under the car, she gave a couple of very low grunting sounds and they obediently waddled out again and into the deep grass. Unfortunately they went in three directions, and within a minute or two all of them were lost. In some distress now, the mother paced up and down, looking anxiously for them and calling softly, a very low *hunnhh hunnhh*. Hoping for another photograph, we turned our car into the grass and nearly ran over one cub, so we decided to take no further chances and just wait to see what happened. The temptation was very strong to lean out of the door, pick up the cub and wave it at the mother: "Here's one of them, over here," particularly as the infant seemed totally bewildered by the lofty forest he had blundered into. He would poke his nose tentatively through the grass for a few feet in one direction, then give up and sit down. After a minute or so he would try it in another direction. Meanwhile his mother had located two of the other cubs, had carried them to a spot several hundred feet away and apparently told them to stay put. It took her another 20 minutes to find the third. But now she was ranging farther and farther from where the last one was sitting. Her head was low, and we could barely make out her shoulders over the tops of the grass. Carefully we backed a few feet away from the youngster; instantly he was swallowed up by the grass. We waited and waited. The light began to fail. We wanted to be on our way but were afraid to move for fear of hitting him in the gathering darkness, and neither of us was anxious to get out of the car to make sure he had not crept under the rear wheels, because we no longer knew where the mother was. It was well we stayed inside. Suddenly she appeared, shockingly large and silent in the dim light, and plucked her last cub out of the grass almost under our noses. The way she carried him was a surprise to me. I had expected it to be by the neck, as a mother cat carries a kitten. But lion cubs are apparently too heavy for that. This one's head was inside his mother's mouth, held gently there, as in a basket, by her long teeth.

This reunion ended quickly and happily, but others sometimes do not. While John Dominis was photographing the hungry lioness pictured on pages 54-55, she got into a series of bloody scuffles with a couple of males. This so terrified her cubs that they ran away and were not reunited with their mother until three days later. During that time any one of them might have been picked off by hyenas or by a leopard, or might have wandered about until it starved. All in all, a young lion's life is not easy, but the cub makes up for the hazards that confront it by being extremely tough. One litter was found, dreadfully emaciated and dehydrated but still alive, a week after its mother had been shot by a hunter.

There is a postscript to the story of the four cubs that got lost in the grass. I spoke about them the next day to Myles Turner, the Warden at Seronera Lodge, because it seemed unnatural to me that such helpless infants should be found out in the open at all. He explained that the mother was having trouble hunting. The game thereabouts had all moved to another section of the park, leaving her stranded with her cubs. She was even then, when intercepted by us, apparently trying to get them to travel with her to a better hunting locality. This was obviously going to be impossible, and all four of the babies would probably have perished had not Turner made the decision to carry them over by shooting a zebra and leaving the carcass where the mother could find it. A week later he did the same thing, and the last I heard, the four cubs were doing well. I may even have seen them again. I went back to Seronera Lodge five years later and the place was alive with lions. Of the 40 or 50 individuals that I observed then, I like to imagine that one may have been one of those mewing little cubs from under the car, a fine adult now and all unknowing that a considerate warden had pulled him through one of the greatest hazards that can befall a baby lion: a mass exodus of game.

The critical period of infant immobility does not last long. Lions grow rapidly, and at two months they are already big enough and strong enough to begin following their mother. They nurse at every opportunity, happily sucking away until their bellies are as round as melons. I have never tasted lion milk, but since all lion cubs, puppies—and even human babies—tend to have somewhat the same milky smell, it is reasonable to assume that the milk they are drinking is all pretty much the same too. Chemically it is very similar to cow's milk.

The milk requirements of the mother reach their peak when her litter is approaching three months of age. About this time, with the youngsters gaining daily in strength and mobility, they will be introduced to meat. At first the mother will disgorge pieces that she has just eaten. The very brief exposure of the meat to her own internal juices apparently makes it easier for the babies to digest. Later she will bring back a raw hunk from a kill and let the cubs worry away at it on their own. This is an important first learning process. They must become quick and efficient feeders if they are to get more than crumbs from then on, for they will shortly be introduced to other lions.

By the time he is three months old, a cub is a pretty husky specimen. About the size of a spaniel, his body has at last begun to catch up with his head. His tail is beginning to lose its stumpy look and lengthen out a bit, but his paws—by house-cat standards—are still enormous. They seem to grow just as fast as the rest of him, and to the close observer of a young lion the realization will gradually dawn that a lion's paws are just plain big, and always will be big. At about this time also comes the realization that a lion cub is not merely an overgrown kitten. He is an entirely different animal, and big paws are part of that difference. He is no pouncer, no dainty cuffer of mice, but a grabber, a wrestler. His prey, even when he grows up, may be bigger than he is, and he will have to subdue it by brute force. At three months, he is already giving signs of how he will go about this. His shoulders and forelegs are filling out. Playing with a cub, one can feel the strength beginning to flow into those shoulders.

Not long ago I had the pleasure of meeting a three-month-old cub belonging to an American educator, Jane Campbell. Miss Campbell, who had become fascinated by lions while working with the Peace Corps in Ethiopia, had already raised three of them. When they were a year old, and getting too large to handle, she sent them to England where they are now members of a pride that roams a large estate owned by the Earl of Bath. Back in the United States, Miss Campbell bought her fourth lion, a female named Sheba, which she introduced to me. Although a bit shy at first, Sheba was extremely affectionate and playful. But her whole scale of behavior was different from a kitten's. She was slower and clumsier, her toys were larger. She liked to hurl herself on a suitcase, gripping it tight with her forelegs and pancake-sized paws. Her way of making friends with me was to hug my leg and gnaw gently at my kneecap. Her clasp was surprisingly strong, and it was easy to imagine how she would ultimately kill her prey: holding and biting it while keeping her own hind legs firmly on the ground. An adult lion leaping on an antelope tries to keep on its hind feet to maintain its own balance and to drag its victim down.

If three-month-old Sheba had been a wild lion she would already have made the acquaintance of others of her kind. Her mother would either have reentered her own pride or else joined up with one or more lionesses to form the nucleus of a new one. This is a great step forward in the fortunes of young lions. They will have survived the dangerous period of having to lie alone and defenseless in a thicket while their mother is off hunting. Henceforth they will be members of a community. For a while they may be too small actually to tag along during a hunt, but they will not be abandoned; the entire pride does not necessarily go hunting as a unit. An elderly lioness or two, or another nursing mother, may stay behind. So may an indolent male, preferring to take his chances that the kill will be made close at hand and that he will hear the scuffle in time to stroll over and grab his share. One way or another, from now on the little ones can count on big company virtually around the clock.

Being in the pride also makes life easier for the mother because it lightens the burden of hunting. She can share the kills of other lionesses, and she can vastly improve her own chances of killing by getting others to cooperate with her. As will be seen, several adults working together can hunt much more efficiently than a single animal working alone. With this increase of efficiency, of course, the lioness receives the extra dividend of having more time to spare with her cubs.

A third advantage that comes with membership in the pride is that a cub may, in an emergency, find a foster mother. Lionesses are marvelously tolerant, and as long as they have milk to give they will dispense it freely to any hungry cub that comes along. In a large pride there is usually more than one nursing mother at a given time. If one of these should be killed, her orphans may be able to get by on handouts from other lionesses.

This shifting about of youngsters, and the amiability and tolerance shown by lionesses generally, has given rise to the belief that among them exists a class of nurses or "aunties," whose business it is to look after cubs while their mother is away. Over and over again observers have seen lionesses who are clearly not the mothers of cubs, sitting with them, and with obvious indulgence allowing the little fellows to scuffle and wrestle about, rousing themselves only when the play gets too rough. Baby sitters, obviously—or so it was thought by most lion students for a century or more. It has taken the biologist George B. Schaller to explode this idea. Schaller has been conducting an exhaustive study of lions in the Serengeti

(continued on page 61)

Right front pawprint of lion

THE LION

Here is a magnificent specimen of the male lion in the prime of life. Well fed (probably *just* fed, from the barrellike look of his belly), he turns to stare at the camera with that blend of calm detachment and inner menace that only a lion can muster. He has the characteristic head of a male, broader and heavier than the lioness', and made to look even bigger by a fine thick mane that extends down his chest and between his forelegs. Something of the strength that is in him may be seen in the great size of his thighs. They are solid muscle and provide the acceleration he needs for his short, devastating charge. Equally powerful are his upper forelegs, capable of staggering a zebra stallion with one swat. This is a young lion, perhaps four or five years old. He has grown to full size and strength but still shows some of the spots of cubhood. These will fade and disappear as he gets older. He is also lacking in the nicks and scars that an older lion often has, and his back still displays the straightness of youth.

For a great cat, the lion in love can look almost foolishly tender and devoted, his mate calm and inscrutable. During the week that they will spend together they are inseparable. Touch is important. The female is extremely seductive; she will loll in the grass, often with a paw thrown carelessly over her mate's body, or caress him absent-mindedly with gentle swipes of her tail. Spats occasionally occur, like the one at upper right, but they usually consist only of a few snarls. Generally speaking, a mated pair is notably gentle and considerate, and between moments of copulation (which take place several times an hour for long periods) most of their time is spent lazily lying together, yawning, snoozing, leaning comfortably against each other in the simple enjoyment of companionship. If there were another male in the vicinity, the lion's behavior would probably be entirely different. He would be extremely possessive, looking aggressively and suspiciously around, and he might expend a good deal of energy chasing off a rival that in his opinion came too close.

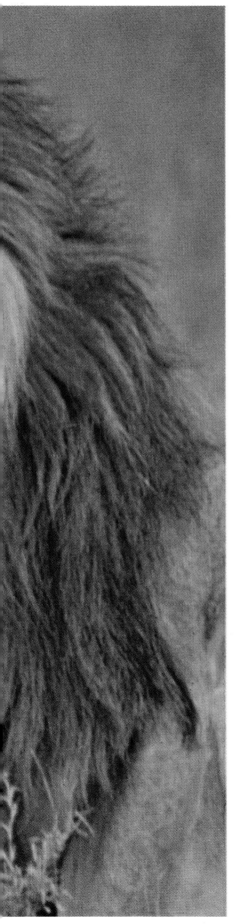

Family life is intimate and affectionate. The cubs have an apparently inexhaustible supply of energy, but their mothers are endlessly patient with them. The males are less so, but even they are remarkably tolerant of youngsters. The sequence at right shows a wise old man about to intercept the saucy spring of an adolescent. He knocks the youngster flat with an easy swipe of his enormous paw, and when he has done this a few times and quieted the cub down he licks him affectionately. Male lions tend to be fretted by the hurly-burly of life in the pride, and some of them prefer to spend much of their time alone (*far right*). Young males often live in bachelor prides and do their own hunting. But in mixed prides the females are the hunters (*next page*).

These two hunting sequences record a success and a failure. In the upper one a lioness has charged prematurely at a herd of zebra. As the first picture clearly shows, she is very thin, probably ravenously hungry, and in her desperation for food has miscalculated badly. The leading zebras are already traveling at top speed across her line of attack and will get clear away, so she swerves (*second picture*) to intercept some of the stragglers, but she slips. In the last picture she has fallen and is hidden in a cloud of dust. Quick to sense their opportunity, the zebras cut behind her, and she gets nothing. In the lower sequence a more experienced lioness has managed to get close enough to a zebra to leap on it. However, her troubles are just beginning. The zebra in this case was big and strong, her grip was not a good one, and she wrestled with it for nearly half an hour trying to get in a lethal bite (*center*) while avoiding its flailing hooves. The battle, waged in the broiling sun, left her exhausted. However, after getting her breath, this lioness did not touch her prey but trotted for several miles to notify her pride that she had made a kill.

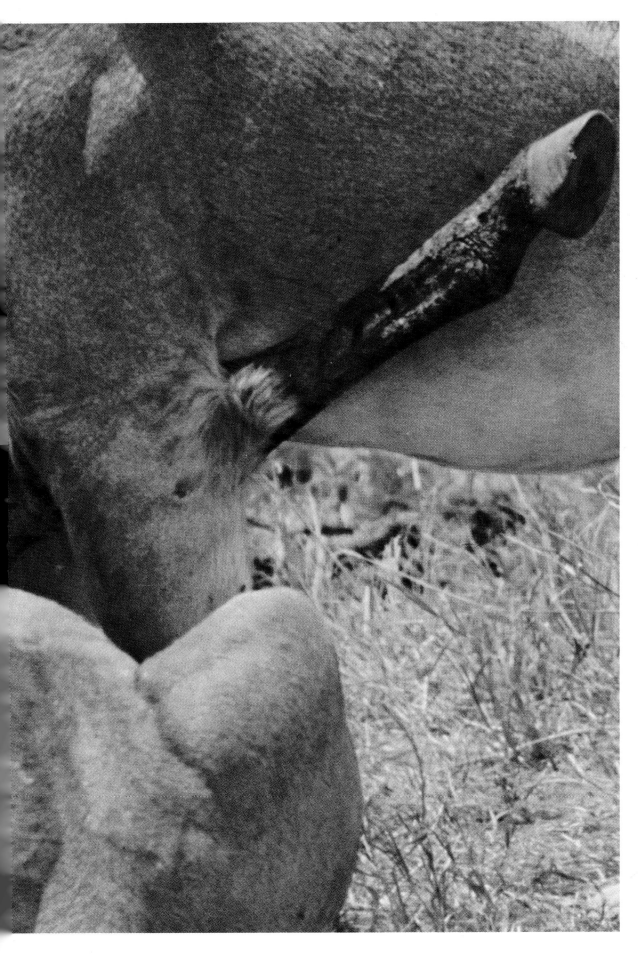

The business of feeding is a nose-to-nose, shoulder-to-shoulder affair in a lion pride, with the larger and stronger animals (if they are hungry or bad-tempered) merciless toward the younger and weaker ones. Under these conditions the youngsters must learn to wait their turn. If they don't they are occasionally killed— and on rare occasions eaten along with the prey. Though most of the hunting is done by the lioness, after a kill her lord and master will stride in and usually feed alone. When he is through, he will move off the kill and permit others to approach it. This picture is not typical, for it shows a male feeding while three lionesses share the meal. When they can eat no more, the members of the pride stroll off one by one, take a drink in a nearby pool or stream and almost immediately fall groggily to the ground and go to sleep (*next page*). Three or four days later the pride will be hungry again, and once more the most active females will be obliged to hunt—like the lioness shown on page 60, starting an evening's prowl under the blue shadows of Mt. Kilimanjaro.

National Park, traveling with two prides and keeping them under almost daily observation for months at a time. He has noticed that aunties do indeed sit with cubs, but the reason is not so much for the sake of the cubs as for the aunties. They know that the mothers, with a need to supply milk to hungry babies, will be active hunters. Therefore, the aunties sit around with the babies, waiting for the mothers to kill—thus insuring themselves of a good chance for food at a minimum of effort.

His introduction to a pride must be a momentous experience for a cub. Up to now he has known only one world, a tiny world of certain familiar tufts of grass, a few bushes and rocks populated only by his littermates and by the enormous and comforting body of his mother. Otherwise there is only the sun and the wind, crickets creaking at night, vultures and eagles soaring overhead by day. There will be little excursions, wobbly walks to new thickets and rocks. Then, one morning, there will be a longer walk than usual, and at the end of it a strong scent, familiar but strange, reassuring but a little frightening too—his mother's scent, but not his mother. Suddenly huge heads will rise up out of the grass. Big, shaggy faces will appear, some even bigger than his mother's, benign but with a hint of menace. Enormous bodies will loom over him. Overcome by timidity, he will huddle close to his mother while these giant strangers inspect him. He will be looked at, sniffed over, licked—all with great gentleness. Adult lions are fond of cubs, and the introduction of some new ones is an occasion for a good deal of solicitous examination. Thus reassured, the youngsters settle in very quickly, and in a few days they may not remember that there was ever a time when they were not surrounded by other lions of all ages and sizes.

Now begins a long period of learning how to be a lion. There is much to learn, and consequently it must come slowly. This means an extended period of "childhood" for the lion, not only to give it time to assimilate the things it must know, but also to ensure that it has plenty of time for play, for it is in play that the mental capacities of higher animals develop. The longer the period of childhood, the greater the intellectual potential of the adult will be. Man, of course, is the extreme example of this. He is the smartest animal known, and his children are the slowest to mature, being literally incapable of surviving by themselves until they are six or seven years old. By contrast, a young wildebeest has little to learn, and consequently learns little. It is able to run after its mother within an hour of its birth, and within weeks—except for nursing—it can take care of itself pretty well. Among lions it takes at least a year to master the rudiments of being a lion, and at two or three years many lions are still learning the fine points of their trade.

Thus, although they grow quickly, lions develop slowly. A three-month-old cub is not as advanced physically as a puppy of the same age. The latter will be better coordinated, quicker and more precise in its movements, and seem just a little brighter overall. This difference in rate of development is highly deceptive, however. Cubs are not less intelligent than pups. Some observers, Jane Campbell for one, think that they are more so. The four lions that she owned were all housebroken with great ease; they quickly learned to open doors with latches, something the average puppy could never do; they were extremely observant, and what they observed seemed to penetrate more permanently than is usually the case with the average slap-happy puppy, who may be better coordinated but whose memory is apt to be short and whose attention span approaches zero.

A lion's early training is mainly muscular. Now that he has joined a pride, he spends his waking hours in almost continuous play. Already he will have picked up—whether by instinct or by observation I do not know—the habit of crouching and stalking. He will do this with his littermates by the hour as they engage in an endless round of wrestling, chewing and chasing. For a while their play, owing to their slow development and to the fact that they are destined to be very large, strong animals, has a curious kind of slow-motion, muscle-bound quality to it. One can almost see a cub turning over in his mind whether or not to jump on his brother—and then deliberately and heavily doing so.

The tail tufts of adults are an endless source of fascination to cubs. The tufts are apt to move unexpectedly and tantalizingly, just enough to catch a youngster's eye. They are also just the right size for combat, reassuringly smaller than the cub himself, hairy little enemy bodies that cannot fight back. You can get right down on the ground with a tail tuft, wrap your legs around it and battle away to your heart's content. It is also good for pulling. If you get a good grip on it you can dig in with all four feet and tug until your muscles pop—without any effect, because there is always a 300-pound animal attached to the other end. The amount of such harassment that adult lions will put up with is amazing, particularly since the teeth of the youngsters are as sharp as tacks, and capable of painful nips. Lionesses thoroughly enjoy the company of cubs, or they would never endure the amount of climbing, tugging, chewing and scuffling that goes on. They almost never swat obstreperous youngsters. If the roughhouse gets too bothersome, a lioness will walk away and continue her siesta in another place.

A mother is particularly solicitous of her own young. Although not appearing to do so, she keeps a close eye on them, and of course she is always there as a sort of fortress that a cub can seek refuge in if he begins to get knocked about by bigger, tougher cubs. Once in the Serengeti I was given a good demonstration of the moral support a mother can give a baby by just being there. A lioness was sprawled on her back, sound asleep, nursing four small cubs. Along came a much larger cub looking for a meal. All four teats being occupied, the intruder decided to bully his way in. He laid his ears back and snarled in a most menacing way at the nearest nurser. But the latter was not to be intimidated. He laid *his* ears back and did his comical best to look fierce while still hanging on to the teat. The bigger cub then tried to push the smaller one aside with his head. Only then did the little one let go, and then only long enough to bite the intruder on the nose. This bold response was so unexpected—as well as painful—that the larger cub fell over himself in his effort to jump away, and the little one went on peacefully nursing. He had had his say: "This is my place, my teat, my mother. You keep off," and he had said it without any backup from his mother. She slept through the incident.

Mothers discipline their young more by guidance than by punishment. This has been eloquently shown in a series of photographs taken of a family of lions by Emmy Haas, and published in a book, *Pride's Progress*. Miss Haas's pride happened to be captives, residents of the Bronx Zoo in New York, but their habitat was a spacious and comfortable one so that, except for hunting, they lived almost as wild lions do. The mother, Princess, was an exceptionally good parent. She was unfailingly gentle with her young, and when they were small she kept a constant eye on them to make sure that they did not fall into a deep trench that surrounded the "island" that they lived on and that separated them from the rest of the world. If a cub seemed headed for the edge, Princess would try to nudge him in another direction. She would do this patiently a number of times, and if he continued to go where she did not want him to, she would place her body in the way. Sometimes she would firmly put her paw on him.

All this play and parental gentleness make the first few months of a cub's life something of a leonine heaven on earth. Schaller has described it as idyllic, and it is, except for one menace that slowly grows and grows. After cubs are introduced to meat, at about three months of age, their requirement for this food increases week by week, and at six or seven months, when their mother's teats begin to go dry, they have to get along entirely on meat. They may not manage it, for at mealtime the other side of

the lion's character manifests itself. A hungry lion is about as directly mo-
tivated as it is possible to be. When food is short, there is a great deal of
elbowing, snarling, snapping and clawing around a kill. Youngsters trying
to worm their way in for a bite get swatted right and left. Even their own
mothers lose their sense of protectiveness by the time her cubs are a year
old and may turn on them. Many are so intimidated by the ugliness and ferocity of their elders that they simply hang around on the outskirts,
hoping that there will be something left for them. If the kill is a large one,
there generally will be, for then the essentially amiable dispositions of
lions assert themselves. A mother may even bring out a few chunks of
meat for her hungry youngsters, but only when her own appetite is thoroughly satisfied. If the hunting is bad and the kill small, they get nothing.
They grow thinner and weaker, and sometimes literally starve to death
while watching larger lions munching away right in front of them.

If they are hungry enough and desperate enough, cubs may risk stepping up to the table before it is their turn. But the risk is great. Guggisberg
mentions one kill made by a group of apparently famished lions. When the
dust had settled five dead cubs were lying on the ground. Such casualties,
however, are not common. On rare occasions the dead young are eaten along
with what they themselves had hoped to eat.

More often than not, however, the hunting is good and the cubs flour-
ish. But the iron beneath the sociability is there, and a youngster must
learn to be quick, opportunistic, patient and respectful. Grown males are
often of uncertain temper, and if there were no way of anticipating their
gruffness and de-fusing it, the carnage in the prides would be devastating,
for inexperienced youngsters would constantly and unwittingly be stumbling
into the jaws of death. How this problem is avoided is very interesting.
All the large carnivores, and many other species besides, are potentially so
dangerous to other, weaker members of their own kind that behavioral patterns must be developed to prevent the stronger ones from killing the
weaker ones whenever they become angry at them. This is invariably accomplished in the same basic way, although the details may vary from
species to species. It is done by signals. The threatened animal immediately
adopts a certain fawning or cringing position, in which it deliberately ex-
poses itself in such a way as to make killing as easy as possible for the
attacker. He, in turn, recognizing the gesture, does nothing. For both animals the action is instinctive. It would have to be, for at moments of
such peril there obviously would be no time for learning by trial and error.

Among wolves, the weaker animal turns toward his attacker in such a way as to expose his throat, saying in effect: "I am at your mercy, you may now kill me if you want to." Among lions, the signal is for the weaker animal to crouch or lie submissively on the ground with its head stretched forward as if inviting a lethal bite in the neck. This action triggers an inhibiting reaction in the attacker. It freezes him; he cannot carry out his threat. The further down the evolutionary scale one goes, the stronger and more reliable these action-reaction combinations are, nor do they always involve threats. Certain frogs cannot distinguish between males and females of their own species. As a consequence, males attempt to copulate with any individual of their kind that hops by. If the target is a female, she submits. If it is a male, he emits a grunt which indicates to the other male that he has his signals mixed. There is no "thought" involved here. One action (grunt) automatically triggers another (leave).

Among animals as highly evolved as lions, the signals work most of the time—as they do among human beings. When two boys are fighting, the one who goes limp and "hollers uncle" is signaling to the other that he is no longer a threat, and it takes a real bully to continue to bash away at him. But as there are bullies among boys, so there are among lions. Amid the complexities of instinct-versus-choice among the higher animals, the issue is not always entirely clear-cut.

The problem of the occasional slipup in reaction, however, is not so important or so interesting as how the attacking animal signals that he is angry. This cue may be so subtle and quick as to be invisible even to a trained human observer. How does the cub know he is in danger? So far, we do not really know, and the depth of our ignorance has been revealed by Emmy Haas in her observations of the pride in the Bronx Zoo. The male in this family was named Charlie, and like Princess he was a model parent. The cubs rolled over him at will and must often have taxed his patience. However he gave no sign of it, and as far as Miss Haas could tell, he had never, by the slightest gesture, given any indication that he was any more dangerous than a sofa pillow. And yet, one day when a cub looked at him, inviting him to play, Charlie responded with such a quick and purposeful bound that the cub flipped itself over instantly and lay in an attitude of terrified submission with its head out. This was an electric moment. Charlie stood over the cowering infant. Princess came up. There was some licking and reassuring, and the incident was over.

But what had Charlie done? His intent was not punitive, it was playful. And yet there was something menacing in the swift way in which he moved that triggered a deep reaction in the little one—a reaction that came faster than thought, gained over thousands of generations of trial-and-error selection until it is now as much a part of every lion as his whiskers.

Lions undoubtedly have many such behavioral cues, and it is responding properly to them that enables them to live sociably despite their potential for destruction of each other. Armed with his instincts, observant, plucky and lucky, a cub will grow up. Weaned at six months, now as big as a collie but considerably heavier and stronger, he is just beginning to show some of the lithe purposefulness of an adult. He will go out hunting now, tagging along with his betters, learning how to stalk and how to kill. As the adults come up on a herd of game they will crouch low and worm their way forward. The youngsters will copy them, but often curiosity will get the better of them. Heads will bob up and the game will scatter. Disgustedly the adults will try again. This time the cubs may be more patient, or perhaps the pride will split, some adults realizing that if they are going to get anything to eat, they will have to shake the young ones.

By the time they are a year old, the youngsters are becoming useful stalkers themselves. And they may already have had some experience in trying to kill. Occasionally a mother will disable a prey animal and let her cubs get some practice in finishing it off. This can be a gruesome business when the young killers are clumsy. I have seen a series of photographs of three husky two-year-olds trying to bring down a wildebeest. One had gotten such a good grip on its muzzle that the prey could not shake loose. The others climbed all over it, biting and clawing for 10 minutes before the wildebeest went down. It was another 20 minutes, during which a good part of it had literally been eaten, before it stopped its struggles.

At one year of age the differences between male and female cubs begin to show and among the males the first wisps of a mane appear. By 18 months the males are noticeably larger, and their heads, shoulders and chests begin to fill out. The mane continues to grow until, by the time he is five or six years old, a male will have a shaggy ruff of hair. It may extend down his back and his chest, some lions even having large tufts on their elbows. There is a great variation in the manes of lions, both as to size and color. Occasionally an otherwise handsome animal in the prime of life will have a puny mane. Colors range from a rich golden to a deep brownish black. "A fine black-mane" is the term often used to describe the epitome of leonine beauty and development, and many people think that black manes are found only in lions that have grown to complete maturity. It is true that in some instances there is a darkening of mane with age, but the idea that all lions will get black manes if they live long enough is false. There are too many scraggly old fellows hanging around with yellow manes for there to be any question about that. Also false is the idea that black manes denote a certain race. Lions born in the same litter often have different colored manes.

As they approach two years, males may leave the pride and strike out for themselves, often in the company of other males their own age. They may be lucky enough to find an area containing unattached females and set themselves up as proprietors, or they may drift about, leading a fringe existence until they feel up to challenging an established proprietor.

Females tend to cling more closely to the pride as they mature. But they, too, often drift away. A pride is a flexible thing with intricate comings and goings. There is no fixed set of rules that will cover all the possibilities, and this is because lions themselves are flexible—and highly unpredictable. Any statement made about them must be understood to apply to lions in general. In a given situation one can never be sure how an individual animal will behave. Nursing mothers, for example, are supposed to be fiercely protective of their young, but they are sometimes anything but that. A. R. Dugmore, wishing to photograph a lioness close at hand with her cubs, could not get a picture because the lioness kept retreating into deeper bushes. He finally went up and seized a cub, hoping to provoke the mother, but she still skulked, preferring to abandon her young rather than run the risk of trying to rescue them.

Lions continue to grow until they are about three years old. Even after that they fill out and increase in strength. They reach their physical peak at about the age of four. There they will stay for four or five years, barring accidents, until old age begins to set in. From then on it is all downhill. Their legs become stiff, their reactions slow. Their teeth wear down to stumps, their eyes are not what they used to be. If they live with a pride, they do so on sufferance. More often they are driven away by younger, stronger males. Now hunting becomes a serious problem, and old lions are apt to be hungry a great deal of the time. They become skinny and feeble. Many of them end their days by being killed and eaten by hyenas.

In his prime a lion is a stunning piece of workmanship. He will measure a good nine feet from nose to tip of tail and will weigh as much as 400 pounds. There are occasional reports of record animals that measure 10 and 11 feet, but professionals are skeptical of these claims, since it is possible to stretch and peg a lion skin beyond its usual size while it is still soft and flexible. James Stevenson-Hamilton, who served for many years as warden of Kruger National Park in South Africa, was particularly suspicious of these extra-long specimens. He personally measured more than 150 lions, making a point of doing so with a steel tape measure directly after they were killed, and he found that only exceptional animals measured as much as nine and a half feet. Once shown a skin that was well over 10 feet long, he noticed immediately that this extraordinary length had been achieved at the expense of width, and he observed wryly that this improbable animal "must have looked in life like an enormous but much attenuated weasel."

Female lions are almost always smaller than males. They average eight feet in length and weigh about 300 pounds. In both sexes, much of the weight is taken up by muscle, which lies in thick ropes and bands all over the animal's body and never fails to impress the man who first skins a lion. A lion's muscles are enormous, their very size serving as anatomical proof of what so many different eyes have seen lions do. Despite their heavy bodies they are remarkable jumpers. One man claims that he saw a male jump across a 36-foot gorge without an instant's hesitation, although the gorge was more than 70 feet deep. Vertical leaps of 10 feet up banks or over hedges are made with ease, propelled by hind legs of explosive power. The forelegs are, if anything, stronger. The forearm is as big as a big man's thigh. It can knock 400 pounds of zebra off its feet with one swat. Jaw, neck and chest muscles are in proportion, and make it possible for a lion to drag large carcasses, sometimes—as reported by Guggisberg—with other lions hanging onto them. Guggisberg has also turned up an account of two males that dragged a dead horse uphill through thick brush, "a feat of strength which would have required the efforts of twenty men."

The purpose of all this strength is, of course, hunting. The day-in and day-out diet of lions is the medium-to-large antelopes such as impala, waterbuck and wildebeest, as well as zebra. All of these animals are common, particularly wildebeest. They are large enough to provide a good meal for a group of hungry hunters, and yet not so large as to exhaust the hunter or endanger his life. Therefore they are the preferred prey, but they do not begin to exhaust what lions eat. They have been seen feeding on grubs, rats, fish, birds, foxes, porcupines, pythons, crocodiles, buffaloes, rhinos, giraffes—and people. A lion, in short, will eat anything made of meat, and the meat does not have to be fresh.

The larger prey animals are tough customers. Buffalo are regarded by some as the meanest animals in Africa. Many hunters consider them to be more vicious, more vindictive, less predictable and, when wounded, more dangerous than lions themselves. They may weigh over 1,500 pounds and travel in large, mutually protective herds. And yet lions go after them, often succeeding in cutting calves from the herd as it stampedes by. A single buffalo in the prime of life is a match for any lion, but not for a hunting pair. One will engage its attention up front while the other lunges in for a crippling bite from behind. Hamstrung, or with a broken leg, the buffalo is then quickly overcome.

Hippos are occasionally taken on in the same way, but they are not usually subdued unless they are young. At night they come out of the rivers to eat grass, and lions sometimes find them browsing as much as a mile from the water. They would seem to be about as vulnerable as tanks. Their hides are as much as two inches thick in places and lined with deep layers of coarse fat. Their legs are short and stout but capable of surprising speed. Under a full head of steam a two-ton hippo can chug along at 20-25 miles an hour and carries about as much authority as a freight locomotive. It has a fearsome jaw with 20-inch tusks that can take a man's leg off with one bite. Why lions would pick on this animal is hard to imagine unless they were extremely hungry, but they do. Stevenson-Hamilton writes of a large bull hippo that was attacked one night by three lions at some distance from the water: "The noise was deafening, and all the details of the struggle could be distinctly heard at the camp, over half a mile distant. In the morning it was clearly indicated how the hippo had trudged along, until the water was reached, carrying the lions on his back, or dragging them after him as they made unavailing attempts to get their claws through his skin."

These dramatic encounters are exceptional. Where the herds of wildebeest and zebra abound, the lions dine almost exclusively on them. Their hunting methods have been studied and described countless times, and although observers disagree on the amount of cooperation and skill that the pride exhibits, there is no question that there is a good deal of it.

Watching the start of a hunt evokes mixed feelings—of thrill and foreboding—in the human beholder. In open country, where the cover is sparse, the hunt usually begins at dusk because the keen eyesight of antelopes makes them hard to stalk during the day. On the Equator the sun drops straight down to the horizon, and twilight is short. As the darkness falls, it envelops the herd that the hunters have kept under idle observation half a mile away. Suddenly the herd is no longer visible, but it is still there, alert now, uneasy. And the watcher cannot help putting himself in the place of the members of that herd, one of whom is about to be killed.

What goes on in the mind of a wildebeest as it stands in the cool darkness, so refreshing after the dust and the heat and the flies of noonday, but so menacing now in its silence? There are lions around. There are always lions around; they are as much a part of life as breathing. During the day they were seen, watched from close by without fear, for a seen lion is a harmless lion—it can be outrun. But it is dark now, and that shivery lion scent is drifting on the air. The night's forfeit will be taken, and if not tonight, tomorrow night. Meanwhile, listen carefully. Attend to the gentle breathing, the occasional soft snort of the herdmates scattered all around you; if they are safe, so are you. Draw deeply of the breeze, beware of shadows, any shadows. Is that a tuft of grass? Was it there a moment ago?

As they move off toward the herd, the members of the pride, so recently relaxed and playful, are now implacable, stepping out silently, one by one. In the dark all cats are gray, and these cats, big as they are, vanish like gray smoke after a few paces. The first to go are the adult females, fanning out in an irregular line. Then come the cubs, alert, bouncy, often doing a great amount of rolling in the grass as they go. Last may saunter the males. Their role is often equivocal. Sometimes they do nothing, apparently anxious only to keep in touch with the harder-working lionesses so that when the kill is made they can quickly take possession of it. At other times they cooperate. They may wait until the females have circled around behind the herd. Then with a few low grunts they move in and stampede the prey into the jaws of their waiting partners. Then comes a moment's frenzy of flying shapes and thudding hoofs, a gigantic spring, a gurgling blat, a crash and a cracked neck. The rest of the herd thunders off to reassemble, the night's agony over. The adrenalin slows. Hearts can beat normally again.

Having been victims of this kind of stalking and stampeding countless times, the antelopes are very wary of it, but the trouble is that if the lions that are going to spring the trap are well hidden, the antelopes do not know which way to run—particularly at night. But many of them seem to know, either from experience or instinct, that they should not run directly away from the apparent danger. They resist being herded, and this is very apparent—to me, at least—during the day when they are disturbed by automobiles. Sometimes in the Serengeti the herds of wildebeest, zebra and Thompson's gazelle extend to the horizon, and the driver of a car feels as if he were in a ship, cutting a wake through an endless sea of animals. But unlike waves of the sea, the waves of animals do not part and ripple off to a respectable distance on either side of the approaching car. Rather, the animals begin to run parallel to it, close alongside, faster and faster, and then putting on an extra burst of speed in order to cross in front. I believe that this peculiar trait is an expression of the antelopes' uneasiness about being cut off and driven back to some as-yet-unrevealed danger. They prefer to run with the car, and sprint around it to safety, away from where they think the car is herding them. They never seem to notice that there are as many gazelles on the other side, also desperately sprinting to cross over to what they, too, believe to be safer ground.

Lions are by no means infallible hunters, and as John Dominis points out in his foreword to this book, they often seem to behave with incredible stupidity. The male may mess up a long and carefully prepared stalk by blundering forward too soon; cubs will betray their presence by bobbing up for a look, or often by rushing forward while still out of range. For these reasons, and because of the extreme wariness and speed of the game, many stalks end unsuccessfully. Just because there is plenty of meat around does not mean that every lion stomach will be full. When there is a foul-up, the lions simply keep on hunting, and an experienced pride will kill regularly and with a minimum of effort. Depending on its size, it may do this every two to four days. Careful records have been kept by observers in both East and South Africa, and these indicate that the average lion eats somewhere between 10 and 20 average-sized antelopes a year. This is far lower than many earlier estimates would have had us believe. These ranged from 60 up to 300 kills per lion per year, and were patently ridiculous considering that a captive lion eats less than 20 pounds of meat a day. Wild ones, leading more strenuous lives, eat considerably more, but even so, this can only add up to 10 or 15 wildebeest per year—at 400 pounds per wildebeest—after making allowance for the weight of the bones. Whether a lion hunts alone or with a pride, the same method of bringing down the quarry is usually employed. In either case, the hunter must somehow get close enough to its prey to close with a rush and drag it down. A lion has great initial takeoff, and in a couple of bounds is moving at a speed of about 30 miles an hour. If it starts from within 50 yards, and can get in that all-important first jump before the victim jumps, it generally can catch it. Ranging alongside, the lion makes a leap for the shoulder, usually hooking one paw around the muzzle and tugging back on it. This jolting impact, slamming into a desperately running antelope, will usually bring it down on its face with such force that its neck will be broken. If it is not, the lion then tries to finish it off by biting it in the neck or throat.

Speed, strength and skill are all necessary here, for a zebra or wildebeest is as heavy as a lion and will fight desperately for its life. If it can struggle to its feet it may, with a couple of vicious kicks, be able to break out of the lion's grip and, if it has not been seriously injured in the initial contact, can even escape. Unsuccessful encounters of this kind happen most frequently to inexperienced young males who may even occasionally wind up with shattered jaws or serious horn wounds. They may be strong enough and swift enough to close with a prey animal, but not always experienced enough to dispatch it quickly. Even a wise and efficient adult may have trouble. The lioness shown at the bottom of pages 54 and 55 was unfortunate in not breaking the neck of her victim with her first onslaught. There then ensued a 30-minute struggle that left the lioness completely exhausted by the time her victim expired.

A stalking lion must gamble everything on its initial charge. If it starts its rush from a few yards too far away, or at a moment when its prey is looking at it, the intended victim will be off like a shot. All antelopes can outrun lions, and any time the hunter realizes that he is not narrowing the gap, he gives up after a few bounds. Surprisingly, the antelope will often stop too, and will sometimes even walk back toward its pursuer, preferring to remain close enough to keep an eye on it, and knowing precisely how close that can be. The hunted also seem to know when the hunters are hungry, and it is remarkable to see how unconcernedly they will graze near dozing lions. But if they have any reason to suspect that the lions mean business they are extremely alert. One often finds a mixed herd of antelopes all staring fixedly at the same spot. What are they looking at—an anthill or a few stalks of grass? Apparently nothing, but moving closer, an observer may find a lion hiding in a bit of cover that one would think too small to conceal a jackrabbit. It is astonishing how those big tawny bodies can flatten out and disappear. The black edges of their ears break up the contours of their faces, and the ridges of hair along their backs look like blades of grass. If a lioness thinks herself unseen, she will lie utterly still, sometimes for half a day, waiting patiently for a small herd of zebra out on the plain to come by on their way to the water hole.

But the zebras are patient too, and very wary. Despite the sun they stand out there for hour after broiling hour, their bodies seeming to wriggle and dance in the heat waves that rise from the baked ground. Tails swish like metronomes at the flies that follow all animals in Africa and seem to increase exponentially as the sun burns down harder and harder. Will the zebras never move?

Sooner or later they will, and the experienced lioness waiting for them knows it. Slowly, imperceptibly, they drift closer, cautious, nervous—but thirsty. Furthermore, if they are going to drink, it is much safer to do so during daylight. The lioness knows this too. She has even figured out the path they will probably follow. She has chosen an innocuously small piece of concealment, guessing that the zebras will prefer to pass pretty close by it rather than risk the more obvious danger of that deeper thicket over on the other side.

She has guessed right. As they narrow the range, stepping faster now in order to get in for a few sips and get out again, she tenses her legs beneath her. Suddenly the zebras stop. Have they scented her, or is this only super-caution? They are now so close that a younger lion, unable to stand the strain, would almost certainly leap out after them. But the old girl is wiser and infinitely patient. Another dozen yards and they will be hers. Again she is right; the cautious mincing march is resumed, and at just the right moment she launches herself like a yellow projectile. Enormous claws curl across the flaring nostrils of a plump stallion and gather him in.

A nursing mother hunting alone to support young cubs may have her kill all to herself. But most lionesses have connections; like poor cousins at Christmas, they show up. One of the first to arrive, if he is close enough at hand to realize that a kill has been made, will be the dominant male. Up he trots, and any others who may have arrived before him give way. He will eat what he wants and, depending on his disposition, may allow others to share the kill while he is still on it. However, more often than not he prefers to dine alone.

Hildebrand, the Nairobi lion mentioned earlier in this chapter, was a particularly hoggish animal. Guggisberg watched him one day, stuffed with food, lying next to a half-eaten wildebeest. A lioness had killed the animal but had not gotten any of the meat, and now she and her cubs were sitting 50 yards away waiting hungrily for their turn. "Even that," says Guggisberg, "was too near for Hildebrand—he half got up, growled threateningly, and the whole family fled a hundred yards or so." Hildebrand then went for a drink in a nearby pool. "Hardly had he turned his back on the kill when the three cubs came trotting towards it in a wide circle. The fastest one reached the carcass ahead of its companions and hastily started tearing at the meat. Hildebrand immediately noticed that something was going on. . . . Uttering a fierce growl, he swung round and came tearing through the grass. With his big paw he hit at the rash youngster, which threw itself on its back. . . . After growling for a while, Hildebrand caught hold of the kill . . . as if he had not eaten for several days, and his belly began looking more and more like a balloon."

The cub took this opportunity to get away, but he and his brothers "did not give up all hope of a meal. Making themselves as flat as possible, they inched their way towards the kill, running a few steps whenever the old gentleman happened to look to the other side. When they were only a few yards away from their goal, Hildebrand uttered an occasional warning growl, and each time the little ones made themselves even flatter. They actually rolled over on to their sides and behaved as if they were asleep. One of them finally reached the wildebeest and began to eat." Here is as good an account as could ever be found, by a trained observer, of the combined hardships and temptations encountered by ravenous young lions when hunger prods them into testing the uncertain tempers of their greedy elders.

But old Hildebrand, despite his bad manners, was not really "greedy"; it is improper to give those man-made labels to animals. Lions habitually eat as much at a sitting as they can because it is never certain when they will eat again. Any attempt by other lions to move in and get any of "their" food stimulates them to see if they cannot cram down a little more themselves before giving it up.

The amount a big lion can hold is remarkable: 40 or 50 pounds of meat at one meal, and another 20 or 30 pounds the next day—if there is still that much left on the carcass. Most lions proceed to their feast in much the same way. They first lick up any fresh blood. Then they bite their victim open in the lower belly and remove the organs. Liver, kidneys and heart are preferred and are eaten first. The intestines and stomach are usually dragged aside and, for some interesting but unknown reason, an attempt is often made to bury them. Sometimes this is actually accomplished, sometimes there is a mere ritual scraping of the ground. The animal then returns to the carcass and gets to work on its tissues. Huge hunks of meat are torn off and swallowed, hide and all. The hairy skins of many game animals are tough and thick, and take days to digest. Hunters have examined the stomach contents of many lions that they have shot and have reported large pieces of skin in varying stages of digestion, suggesting that they have come from different animals probably eaten several days apart. Although no scientist—to my knowledge—has commented on this, it occurs to me that the very slowness with which these tough hides are digested may stand a lion in good stead. He may be able to call on a small reserve of slowly digesting protein in a time of unsuccessful hunting.

When the lion has gorged himself, and even during his gorge if he happens to be an amiable character, the others will group themselves around the carcass in a ring, crouched on their bellies, holding a leg or a rib down with a paw while tearing at the flesh with their teeth. As they fill themselves up, with gory faces and sagging bellies, one by one they walk off for a drink, if there is water nearby, then flop down near the kill to sleep off their heavy meal. Now is the time for hyenas, jackals and vultures to arrive. If the lions are absolutely stuffed and feeling very sleepy, hyenas will be allowed to approach. More often they will be chased off. This game may go on for hours, with a lion wishing to settle down for a nap, and getting more and more fretful at having to dash out in the hot sun time after time to guard his kill. Sometimes he will drag it into the bushes with him; sometimes he will simply give up and let the hyenas finish it.

In areas where hyenas are numerous, particularly in the Ngorongoro Crater, which contains a permanent population of more than 400 of these creatures, a big band of them may actually succeed in driving a single lioness off a kill—but never a full-grown male. The whole hyena-lion relationship is an exceedingly complex and interesting one that science is only now beginning to unravel. Hyenas have long been thought to be stinking, skulking, cowardly scavengers. It now turns out, as a result of studies being made in the Crater by the Dutch biologist Hans Kruuk, that hyenas have an elaborate social structure based on large bands that get together nightly for purposes of cooperative hunting. Hyenas are no mere scavangers; they are resourceful and determined hunters in their own right. They are highly observant, and watch the herds constantly in an effort to detect the slower animals—the young, the disabled, or the pregnant cows.

Whether Ngorongoro Crater is a special case, because of the plentiful game that roams its 100-square-mile floor and because of the very high concentration of hyenas there—the highest in the world—is not clear. But in this one place, at least, the hyena does much if not most of its own killing. It is the lion that is the parasite. Hearing the scuffle of some hyenas pulling down an antelope, he jumps out and takes the kill away from them. They may have invested several miles of hard running in their prize, but there is nothing for them to do but depart, breathing heavily, and start again. Or they may hang around for the leavings. Their feeding habits are somewhat different from a lion's, and if they can get to a carcass, they can find things to eat in it that a lion will disdain unless famished. The lower legs of antelopes are pretty stringy, but hyenas will eat them. They have enormously powerful jaws and are adept at cracking bones for their marrow. In fact they grind up so many pieces of bone in the course of their feeding that their dung is nearly white—unlike that of any other mammal.

And in the end they will get their own back from the lion. When he is old, half-starved and no longer able to take care of himself, a day will come when he will find them gathered around him in a ring, hollow-eyed, waiting. He may make a few feeble charges at them, or manage to back himself into some rocks where they cannot get at his hindquarters, but it will be only a matter of time. He may have killed a dozen or more hyenas in his day—rash young ones that may have crowded him ever so slightly, being inexperienced in the terrible swiftness of his paw, and each a cautionary lesson that surviving hyenas never forgot. But it is the survivors that are gathered now. A snap here, a feint there. Some dreadful growls, a last sally, and suddenly they are all over him. He dies as they eat.

This is not a pleasant way for a lion to end his life, but it is better than stretching it out. Lions go hard, and if hyenas do not get to them, they may spend a long time, slowly, wretchedly, starving to death. They are stubborn and resourceful. They eat rats, even swarms of locusts. Some of them learn to watch the sky for gatherings of vultures, a sure sign that there is something dead or dying on the ground below that an old fellow may get a share of if he arrives in time. Starving lions will go to any length to find food, and will even take on porcupines, although this is usually a losing game. A pack horse was jumped one night in South Africa by a lion but, surprisingly, shook off the charge with ease. The owner of the horse shot the lion and found it to be in the last stages of starvation, its paws full of porcupine quills and so puffed up with infection that the poor animal obviously had been scarcely able to walk, let alone hunt.

It is the old and the infirm that most often come into contact with man. No longer able to take wild game, with hunger getting the better of their discretion, they will begin scrounging around human settlements. Stevenson-Hamilton once noticed that dogs were disappearing from his station—as he thought, to hyenas. He put a game ranger in a car one night and tied a dog to a fence in front of it. When something came to take the dog, the ranger shot it and discovered it was a lioness, so badly injured in the back as a result of a previous fight that she could not hunt properly. She had been supporting herself and her cubs on Stevenson-Hamilton's dogs.

Lions also catch chickens, goats and sheep and have a long history of predation on cattle. Once they get a taste for cows they can become a real menace to the African pastoralist. Herdsmen routinely shut up their stock at night inside high thorn hedges, but these are no real deterrent to a hungry pride. Lions are perfectly capable of jumping over hedges six or more feet high; the literature is full of accounts of their doing just this—and jumping out again with a cow held in the jaws. According to more reliable accounts, what usually happens is this: a few members of the pride pace up and down just outside the hedge, counting on their nearness and the rankness of their scent, intensified by one or two faint but suggestive grunts, to stampede the cattle through the hedge on the opposite side of the corral, where other lions will be waiting. If this stratagem does not work, a lion will begin scratching at the hedge, and will finally poke his way through. Once inside, he will then try to grab and kill something. This usually sets off a human uproar, and the startled lion will be seen jumping over the hedge in his haste to get out. Not with a cow, however. Lions do not leap around with prey animals, they drag them.

Nor do they roar, as some think, to stampede game. Lions prefer to hunt in silence. Their roaring is a social or territorial utterance, a proclamation of power and proprietorship. As Armand Denis puts it, a roaring lion is simply saying: "I am a fine fellow; this is my domain." And his proclamation carries far, up to five miles on a still night.

It is the inability to hunt properly—often because of old age—that may turn a lion into a man-eater. Despite his reluctance to tangle with human beings in daylight, he may come across a lone woman working in a field, and in his extremity he may attack her. When he finds out how easy it was, he may take to hanging about on the lookout for another victim. Unfortunately this drain on the local population is not always noticed immediately, and the lion may make off with three or four people before a man realizes that his wife has not spent the night with a sister, or before a child is missed by his mother. Then the men in the tribe sharpen their spears, get their dogs and go to work. If they have a tradition of lion hunting, they can usually run down and dispatch their quarry in routine fashion; man-eaters, by their very calling, are not the best of lions.

Lionesses with cubs sometimes turn to humans when made desperate by the mass departure of game. The same migration that stranded the four cubs mentioned earlier in this chapter had its grimmer side. There is a camp site near Seronera Lodge, and only a few days before my visit in 1962 two men were spending some nights there in a tent. One evening they neglected to zip up the tent fly, and during the night one of the men was wakened by a muffled groan. He turned on his flashlight and saw his friend being carried out of the tent, his head in a lioness's mouth. He jumped up with a yell and succeeded in startling the lioness so that she dropped her victim and ran off. Seronera maintains radio contact with Nairobi, and a plane was sent immediately, but the camper had been so savagely bitten that he died en route to the Nairobi hospital. Needless to say, when my wife and I were camping at that same spot five years later, we zipped up our tent flap every night.

If that lioness had succeeded, she might have tried again, and it is that kind of success, accidentally achieved by a healthy animal, that can get man-eating started in a district that lacks firearms or where the local inhabitants are too scarce or too timid to hunt down the man-eater in reprisal. Once the habit is established it is hard to break, as one lion learns it from another —none of them realizing that man is more dangerous than he seems. Such a situation developed at the turn of the century in Tsavo in southern Kenya during the building of the railroad from Mombasa to Uganda. Large numbers of laborers were imported from India to work on the road-bed, and the British engineer in charge, John H. Patterson, had been on the job only a week when he was told that two of his coolies had been taken out of their tent during the night by lions. At first he disbelieved this story, for his road gang was a mixture of Hindus and Muslims, and since there was a great deal of hard feeling between the two groups, he felt it likely that humans, rather than lions, had done the dirty work. His suspicions were strengthened by the assurances of the coolies themselves that the lions were actually the spirits of dead African chiefs who objected to the building of the railroad across their territory and that it would be fruitless to try to kill these supernatural beings.

Supernatural or not, Patterson got quick proof that he was dealing with lions and not murderers, for a few nights later another coolie was taken. This time it was from a tent containing half a dozen occupants, who watched with horror as a lion suddenly stuck its head in the opening and seized the nearest man by the throat. He had only time to scream, "Let go." The next moment he had been pulled outside and the others were left listening to the gruesome sound of their friend being chewed to death just outside the tent opening.

The next day Patterson verified the story by looking at the pug marks of two lions around the tent, and by following a bloody path to the remains of the unfortunate man. All that was left of him were a few bones and his head, the latter neatly bitten off and the eyes still open.

Patterson resolved to kill the lions, and in the ensuing weeks he spent many nights in trees overlooking tethered goats. He would sit there hour after hour in a cloud of mosquitos. Suddenly from the tents down the

track would come a burst of screams, and he would realize that the lions
had struck somewhere else. He built a large trap and baited it. No luck.
More nights in trees. More screams, more deaths. Finally the camp was de-
moralized, the men refused to work, and all construction came to a halt.
As Patterson tells it: "For the next three weeks practically nothing was
done but build 'lion-proof huts' for those workmen who had had sufficient
courage to remain. It was a strange and amusing sight to see these shelters
perched on the top of water tanks, roofs and girders—anywhere for safety—
while some even went so far as to dig pits inside their tents, into which
they descended at night, covering the top over with heavy logs of wood.
Every good-sized tree in the camp had as many beds lashed on to it as its
branches would bear—and sometimes more. I remember that one night
when the camp was attacked, so many men swarmed on to one particular
tree that it came down with a crash, hurling its terror-stricken load of shriek-
ing coolies close to the very lions they were trying to avoid. Fortunately
for them, a victim had already been secured, and the brutes were too busy
devouring him to pay attention to anything else."

By this time the lions had grown bolder, sometimes taking two victims
in a night, going from tent to tent and braving fusillades of rocks and
sticks while looking for prey. But with most of his men now in tall trees or
stockades, Patterson himself became a target for the interests of the lions.
One dark night when he was sitting on a flimsy platform only a few feet
from the ground, he suddenly realized with a shock that one of the lions
was stalking him. For nearly two hours he was able to follow its movements
by the faintest of rustlings and by the silencing of crickets in the grass as
the lion slowly circled the platform. All this time Patterson could see nothing. With his eyes nearly bursting from his head, he had to wait for a
glimpse of the animal that he knew was coming after him. Finally he spotted it and got off a hasty shot. Roars and loud groans indicated that he
had hit it. He continued to pump bullets in the direction of the lion, and
finally silenced it. The next day he followed its trail and found its carcass.

A few days later he got the second lion, wounding it from a platform during the night. For 10 days he looked for it, finally tracking it down in the
deep brush. There the wounded lion charged him. He emptied one gun
into it without stopping it, and reached for his other, only to find that his
gun-bearer had gone up a tree with it. So Patterson legged it for the tree
too, making it by a jump or two only because the lion was handicapped
by a broken leg sustained on the first volley. The lion retreated again, and
Patterson, retrieving his gun, killed it.

This ended the depredations of the infamous man-eating Tsavo lions. All together, they had killed and eaten 28 Indians, plus, as Patterson the paymaster put it, "scores of unfortunate African natives of whom no official record was kept."

It is unlikely that anything like the Tsavo experience will occur again. The circumstances under which the man-eaters operated were exceptional: early success against a new kind of prey, large numbers of that prey readily available, and apparently defenseless. The lions probably stalked their victims out of habit, not realizing how easy they were to catch, and were obviously contemptuous of their ability to strike back. The only lions in Africa today that could develop a comparable contempt for man are those protected in parks. As long as the humans who watch the lions stay in their vehicles and do not give the lions a chance to find out how good they are to eat, there should be no trouble. What the long-term results will be for those who like to camp out in the reserves is a subject for interesting speculation. Thanks to the Masai, to other spear-bearing tribes and to weapon-bearing white hunters, there still seems to be a tendency among lions—at least during daylight—to avoid humans, so long as the encounter is a casual one not involving cubs, food or sex. At night the rules change. Lions are much bolder. Their natural curiosity often takes them into camps. My own safari friend, Bob Lowis from Nairobi, remembers an evening in the Mara Reserve when his tent began to tremble. He peeked out and found several large cubs playing with the tent ropes and gnawing at the pegs. Fortunately they got bored before the tent came down, and walked away. Another time he became aware of a large bulge in the side of his tent and realized it was the backside of a lion leaning against the canvas.

Such odd and unexpected encounters between lions and humans are bound to increase as the aplomb of the lions grows and as the number of humans in lion country increases. And although this will create problems, there is one man who certainly feels that the problems are more than worth it, just for the satisfaction of knowing that there are still lions living free on their ancestral lands. That man is Mervyn Cowie, the father of Kenya's park system. Cowie grew up in Nairobi, the son of an English sportsman who spent a great deal of his time killing big game, and as a youngster, Cowie himself had ambitions to become a white hunter. But very early in his career he realized that he was much more interested in live animals, particularly lions, than he was in trophies. He also realized that nobody else in and around Nairobi had the slightest concern for lions, which were universally regarded as vermin. "Bash the bastards," was what he heard from every farmer or stockman he met. It became clear to him that unless someone raised a voice in behalf of the lions they would vanish from that part of the world. It also became clear that that somebody would have to be himself. So, without money, without backing, without any more influence than any respectable minor member of the white establishment in Nairobi could muster, he began. The story of his efforts is well told in his book, *I Walk With Lions*. The title is an apt one, for Cowie came to know lions well. As a young man he lived with his parents about 10 miles out of town and used to commute to an accountant's job by motorbike. Coming home in the late afternoon on the lonely tracks that were the forerunners of today's cement highways, he would occasionally see a pride sitting by the road. One such encounter led to an extraordinary dilemma. As Cowie tells it: "I was chugging along in the rain slowly and carefully, skidding on every muddy turn, when my interest was attracted by a family of seven lions, sitting on a bank some eighty yards above the road. So intrigued was I with this scene that I missed my pathway, and the motorbike slipped over onto its side. Worse still, my foot was caught underneath in such a way that I could not move it, nor could I get up to lift the heavy bike. After struggling for some time, I realized it was quite hopeless, and merely thanked my luck that my leg was not being scorched by the hot engine.

"This was too much for the lions, and they became fascinated by a human being in a most undignified position, struggling on the road. I was not very impressed with their decision to come closer for a proper inspection. First one stalked forward a few yards and sat down, and then the rest followed to form a new front line.

"Curiosity was their main motive, but I was not very sure this would be the rule in the hours of darkness. I tried to work out what to do. There was no siren on my motorbike, as I relied on the noisy exhaust to announce my presence. There was no way of sounding an alarm except by shouting. I thought it better to keep silent and still until the lions got really threatening, and then to give them a sudden fright. This I hoped would convince them that I was a proper human being worthy of some respect, even if my leg was entwined under my *piki piki,* as the Africans called it. I began to realize that I was in a nasty predicament, as the lions grew more aggressive in the failing light. One lioness walked around below wind, and had a good sniff at the combined scent of sweat, gasoline and a joint of meat strapped in the saddle bag for the family dinner.

"At this stage I resorted to my prearranged plan of a sudden movement and a lot of shouting. To my dismay, it had little effect. Several of the lions drew back a few yards but gave no sign of a general retreat. Strangely enough, in these circumstances one never seems to accept the inevitable, and I couldn't believe that one of the lions would spring at me.

"Suddenly all the lions jerked to the alert position, on their haunches, but instead of looking at me, they fixed their gaze on the road behind me. By craning my neck in the same direction, I could just make out the dark forms of six Africans walking toward me down the muddy road. I let out another shout, and this time the lions made off into the undergrowth. My saviors turned out to be some Masai. . . . They had heard my earlier shouts at the lions, and had abandoned a short cut to investigate the noise."

Cowie has had other curious encounters with lions. On another afternoon on the same motorbike, he stopped to burn off some grass at the edge of the track and found himself staring into the blazing eyes of a lioness, her muscles tensed and twitching, ready to spring at him from about 15 feet away. Paralyzed by terror, he stood motionless. The lioness snarled, waiting for any movement to trigger her spring. Still he stood. She gradually calmed down—and walked away!

Another hair-raiser grew out of his efforts to get a game sanctuary established near Nairobi. One of the things he liked to do, to whip up local interest, was to show lions to distinguished visitors—for by this time the species had become so scarce locally that a sight of an honest-to-goodness wild lion around Nairobi was something to talk about. Having located three males living in a certain spot, he determined to keep them there for display purposes, and he made a practice of shooting a zebra at regular intervals and trucking it out to where the lions would find it. Unfortunately one of the three lions was bullied by the others at mealtime and never got enough to eat. One afternoon Cowie was driving slowly along, a zebra carcass and two African helpers in the back of his truck, as he turned over in his mind how to provide for the cowardly lion. But that animal solved the problem for him. Having learned that Cowie's truck was where the food was coming from, it was waiting, and in an effort to get ahead of its two companions, it jumped in the back as Cowie drove slowly by. There was a shout, and Cowie looked behind him "to see a vision of a full-grown lion, two people, and a lot of fresh meat jumbled together in the back of the car." Naturally enough, Cowie slammed on the brake, which was the worst thing he could do, for it threw the lion forward on top of one of the cowering Masai helpers. However, the lion was intent only on the meat.

It seized a hunk and jumped out. Cowie's workmen resigned on the spot.

There was nothing Cowie would not do for "his" lions. Observing a mother and small cubs one afternoon, he was puzzled by her repeatedly getting up in some agitation and then lying down again. Investigating this, he came upon one cub that had wandered off. Mewing pitifully, it was walking as fast as it could go in the wrong direction—toward a farm that housed a large number of dogs. He tried to turn the cub around and send it on its proper way, but it was in some distress and would not leave him. He examined it and found a number of fierce-biting safari ants clinging to it. This explained the actions of the family; it had been attacked by the ants and had scattered. But what was Cowie now to do with the cub? It was getting dark—it always seems to be getting dark when a crisis with lions arises—and he could not leave it to the mercies of the farm dogs. So he picked it up and set off on foot toward where he had last seen the lioness. Pretty soon he spotted her coming out of some trees and heading in his direction. He set the baby down and began to back away, but the baby followed, and so did the mother. When she was fairly close she uttered a low mother-lion sound that attracted the infant's attention. It instantly turned and was reunited with her. Cowie felt no alarm during the encounter. He is convinced that the mother had him under observation while he was carrying her mewing, squirming cub, and understood that he meant it no harm. As it turned out, he was right, but such actions are not recommended for people who are not thoroughly familiar with lions and who lack Cowie's quiet skill and confidence in approaching them.

That is where the trouble will come when the human tide of tourists begins to pour into East Africa's game preserves. To date most visitors have known something about wild animals and have had some respect for their idiosyncrasies. Not many are like the English soldier on leave in Uganda's Murchison Falls National Park a few years back. Seeing a large elephant, he did what any unthinking zoo visitor from London might do; he got out of his car and offered it a bun. He was trampled to death.

As the quantity of visitors goes up, the quality of their sophistication goes down; it is bound to. If a real torrent of visitors ever hits the African parks, they may well become like Yellowstone, where the crowds are already too big, and where somebody is always offering pretzels to a bear and donating a few fingers along with the pretzels. Every time an animal kills or seriously injures a human being in a park, that animal has to be destroyed. That is a pity, for it is usually not the animal's fault. It is responding properly to improper behavior on the part of the human.

What the future holds for the lion is hard to say. Forty or fifty years ago one would have had to conclude that it was hopeless. At least the past record was hopeless. For upwards of two thousand years, in one area after another, the impact of human civilization had always ended with the disappearance of the lion, and until recent decades there had been no hint anywhere that this process would not continue down to the bitter end. A few words of history will make this melancholy story very clear.

We tend to think of the lion as a native African animal. He probably originated in Asia, and for a long time was widely distributed throughout Asia and Europe. He was not a tropical animal, but a temperate one, and even possibly a cold-weather one, and he bears witness to that to this day. Cubs are born with such thick fur that they suffer considerably from the heat. Even adult lions dislike the heat. They pant heavily, and seek out shady places to lie up in. Flies bother them immoderately. When the weather turns cool they become animated and frisky. Rain stimulates them, and they engage in licking orgies. I once watched six lions sitting in a circle during a heavy shower, each licking the one in front of it. Nearby, nose to nose, crouched two lionesses, with just room between them for a small cub. It sat facing me, its eyes shut, a beatific expression on its face as two big pink tongues batted its head back and forth like a Ping-Pong ball.

In addition to these physical and behavioral characteristics that suggest a cool-weather origin for the lion is the more compelling evidence of fossils. The caves of Stone-Age man throughout Europe contain lion fossils. Indeed, they contain the fossils of two kinds of lions. One of these was half as big again as the modern lion. It must have possessed awesome powers, but these did not save it from extinction. It gradually became scarcer and scarcer in Europe, and is believed by some experts to have been driven out of existence by human hunters who exterminated the last survivors about two thousand years ago. Others believe that it was a victim of overspecialization and that, like the saber-tooth cat, it failed to compete with the smaller, more adaptable lion of today.

Adaptable as he may be, today's lion is not adaptable enough. He cannot adapt to civilization. At the time of the fall of Troy, lions were common in North Africa, Greece, the Balkans and the Near East. Their range extended through the Middle East and India. Previously it had been even wider, but being open-country animals, lions were compelled to leave large areas by the gradual encroachment of forest following the ice ages. With the tiger (also originally a cool-weather animal) the lion shared the top of the ladder among predators, the tiger taking the forest, the lion the open grassland as his hunting ground. Both have been steadily pushed back by man. Assyrian kings hunted lions from their chariots. Today there are no lions in the Middle East. The Greeks hunted them and so did the Romans in North Africa, and slowly they disappeared from the Mediterranean Basin. It was not only hunting. Changing climate, together with man's disastrous practices as an agriculturalist and herder, have made huge expanses of land unfit for large herbivores. Whether men go to those blighted areas today or not is beside the point—lions no longer live there because there is nothing for them to eat.

The story is the same in India. Bit by bit, lion country was nibbled at by farmers, by drought and erosion, by the disappearance of game, by human crowding and by hunting. Today there is a small population of lions left in India's Gir Forest Reserve, the only lion colony remaining outside of Africa. The 500 square miles of this scrub forest is kept in a reserve by the Indian Government, but the habitat is fast being destroyed by the presence within its boundaries of some 50,000 domestic buffalo cattle and uncounted thousands of goats. The lions naturally prey on the stock, and the Indian herdsmen naturally poison the lions. In 1963 the lion population was down to an estimated 285 individuals. In the intervening years, cattlemen who have been losing cows to the Gir lions have been shooting them. No one knows how many there are left at the moment. Patrolling of the reserve is spotty, prosecution lax, and India is so preoccupied with her human woes that there is no guarantee that this pathetic remnant of a once continent-spanning lion population will get the attention it deserves. How can it? Where will those 50,000 buffalo, those innumerable goats, go? Some conservationists have nearly written off the Gir lions. They are talking about rounding up the survivors and moving them somewhere else.

So there remain only the lions of Africa. And it is largely by accident that they do remain. For humans, Africa is a harsh land. Its droughts, its locust plagues, its diseases have all conspired to keep at bay until very recently the crunch of massive civilizations that developed elsewhere. The cultures that have sprung up within Africa have been ingeniously tailored by their creators for survival there. But the nature of these cultures and the nature of the land have prevented the endemic development of anything on a large scale. Human societies in Africa have been small and specialized, and their reach has been limited. For centuries they have been fractured and static, a crazy quilt of tribes and dialects, with warfare a way of life. In such an environment, modern civilization, with its ability to create cities, to pollute rivers, to turn forest to farm and farm to dust, to crowd and jostle everywhere, simply could not develop. As a consequence, though they have lived with humans for thousands of years, the animals of Africa, by and large, have been unaffected by them. Now the modern world has burst in on Africa so suddenly that it has—in a sense—caught the animals before they could leave. What an extraordinary piece of luck, for if Africa had been capable of developing large-scale civilizations, and had done so over a thousand years or so, as has been the case in Europe and Asia, one may be sure that there would be no more lions around Nairobi than there are around Paris.

This is the marvel of that fantastic African ecosystem—not so much that it is as varied and wonderful as it is, but that it is there at all; that it has endured long enough for us to stumble over it; and that we, the stumblers, at last may be just sophisticated enough—having destroyed similar marvels everywhere else in the world—to make an effort to save this one.

Whether we will succeed or not is another question. But for the first time in human history there are people scattered over the world who are willing to argue the rights of animals against the rights of humans. On how that argument goes in Africa will the future of the lion depend.

THE LEOPARD

For the man accustomed to watching lions, his observations of leopards, if he is lucky enough to have any, will come as a surprise. Considering that both are cats, the differences between the two are extraordinary. It is hard to understand how the largest feline in Africa and the next largest—two animals that often live in the same place and hunt the same prey—can be so totally unlike.

The lion, as noted, becomes a public character if not harassed into secretiveness. He lives comfortably in the full glare of the day. He strolls through life radiating a kind of lazy, lordly power born of the carelessness of authority. He is good-natured and relaxed. He cannot even bother to be graceful. After a large meal he often looks positively awkward, his potbelly sagging and swaying from side to side as he walks. His gregariousness and playfulness are infectious. With good reason he has been called the dog of the cat family.

Not so the leopard, the most catlike of all cats, the quintessential cat. Secretive, silent, smooth and supple as a piece of silk, he is an animal of darkness, and even in the dark he travels alone.

Leopards, because of their furtive habits, are almost impossible to see. "Look for tails hanging down in trees," one is told. "Watch in the thick grass along the dry stream beds; you may catch them at daybreak as they are coming home." On three separate trips to Africa I have looked for tails in thousands of trees, and one chilly dawn after another has found me straining my eyes from the top hatch of a Land Rover jouncing its way along the small watercourses of three countries. How many leopards have looked at me, I do not know, but I have looked at very few of them. The stronger the early morning light gets, the easier it is to see, but as the day grows, so grows the feeling that the leopards (if any) will have hidden themselves. How does one go about looking for an animal that one has never seen? Is a dangling tail all that conspicuous, and how does it compare in size and color with all the tantalizing loops of vine and fig that hang in African trees? There are constant heart-stopping flickers of ground movement along the way, but each turns out to be a duiker or some other small gazelle, or even a francolin, one of the plump partridgelike birds that may be stirring in the thickets. Once, camped at nine thousand feet in a cold beautiful forest on the slope of Mt. Kenya, I found the remains of an antelope in a tree—a leopard kill, but no leopard. I found another antelope, half eaten, in the Mara Reserve early one morning, but there was no leopard there either. We came back that evening and waited until dark, but the leopard did not come. Twice I had glimpses. Once a shape flashed across the track ahead of us and was gone. Another morning in the Mara, Bob Lowis whispered, "There's your leopard." The sun was not yet up, and in the half light all the grass and the bushes looked gray. So did something that shrank back into that grayness—gray into gray—and without appearing to move, vanished.

It was luck, not sharp-sightedness or persistence, that finally broke the drought. Coming back to camp in the Serengeti, after a long and relaxed morning of lion watching, we stumbled under, not over, a leopard in a tree. In full view. Calm and indolent. No problem at all. We drove right up, parked 15 feet away and watched for half an hour, taking pictures and talking in low voices. The leopard paid no attention to us. His tail hung down just as they said it would. He was well fed, with a belly that bulged over the branch on which he lay. His kill, a Thomson's gazelle, was safely wedged in a fork above him. From time to time he looked idly at us, then put his head down on his paws and went to sleep.

Most of the people who know anything about leopards are professional hunters. They are the ones who see them, having baited or trapped them, and consequently much of the information and lore about leopards comes from them. A great deal of it is highly revealing and accurate, but some of it makes little sense. For example, why, if leopards are so shy, do they sometimes lie in trees and let people approach very close to them? In attempting to explain this, some hunters hold that leopards believe themselves to be invisible in trees. Though the idea seems plausible enough, it is incorrect. Leopards certainly feel secure in trees. They are superlative climbers, and are safe from dogs there. And, of course, more often than not they *are* unseen —but that is not the same as being invisible. A leopard will lie motionless in a tree, hoping to avoid detection as an intruder approaches. He freezes, as has often been noticed by Richard Leakey, a Kenya paleoanthropologist who has seen many leopards in the wild. And he may remain frozen if he expects the intruder to pass by without noticing him.

But animals are often quick to realize when they are being observed. The leopard is no exception, and if he suspects that he has been noticed, he probably will unfreeze. He may stand up or move about in the branches. If he thinks the intruder is coming dangerously close, he may even decide to leave. A. Blayney Percival, a Kenya game ranger out with a pack of dogs, once watched his pack tree a leopard. It bounded at the trunk full speed, seeming almost to run about three-quarters of the way up it. Then, as its momentum died, it grasped the bole with its forelegs and rapidly hitched its way the rest of the distance into the lower branches. There it sat, watching the dogs ringing the tree below it. Suddenly it noticed Percival approaching. Without hesitation it started down the tree headfirst, giving a great spring, which carried it out over the heads of the astonished dogs and off into thick bush, where it disappeared. This animal obviously had some knowledge of the hazards of men and firearms and, far from thinking itself invisible, felt dangerously exposed in a tree.

Nevertheless, leopards do sometimes allow themselves to be treed, approached and shot. Is this a belief in invisibility? Almost certainly not. The animal in question may be a young one intimidated by dogs; it may have had no experience with guns, and thus no reason to flee; there may be no convenient bushy cover to flee to. There are many reasons why a treed leopard may choose not to run, and these will vary with the leopard and the circumstances. I believe the individual that behaved in such a relaxed way for me in the Serengeti had probably never been shot at, had met other game-park observers from the safe vantage of a branch and had gradually learned that people did not bother it when it was sitting up there. So, why move?

Many naturalists and old Africa hands have reported that leopards always descend trees headfirst. Is this another old-hunter's tale? Apparently not. Here there is virtual unanimity among observers and good common sense to back it up. To begin with, there is the configuration of African trees. Many of them have their main branches not more than 10 or 20 feet from the ground, and these branches stick out more or less horizontally, rather than soaring upward at a steep angle as is the case with elms, maples and so many other American varieties. Furthermore, the leopard himself is about the nearest thing to an animated steel spring that exists. For his weight, he is markedly stronger and more supple than a lion. A drop of 20 feet is nothing at all to him. Asking him to descend a tree tail first is like asking an able-bodied man to creep laboriously down a flight of stairs backwards.

A tree is home to a leopard. He can jump in and out of it with ease. He can get about in it with remarkable speed and skill, even in small branches, as the pictures on pages 112 and 113 show. It is a place where he is secure from all ground molestation—save that of man. Trees are shady and cool, for if there is any breeze stirring it will be felt in a tree when it may not be detectable on the ground. Furthermore, climbing a tree removes an animal from a great many biting flies and other annoying insects that tend to stay down in the grass or in bushes. It provides a good ambush for leopards that like to do their hunting by dropping on prey animals from branches that overhang game trails. Finally, it serves as a meat safe where the leopard can store the carcass of a kill, away from hyenas and smaller carnivores, which would quickly find and eat it if it were left on the ground.

When not in a tree, a leopard will lie up in a dense thicket during the day, or hide himself in a cool cleft among rocks, depending on the terrain. Leopards may occasionally be picked out with binoculars from a distance as they sun themselves late in the afternoon on kopjes—those majestic piles of ancient rocks that crop up here and there like fortresses on the plains —but by the time the observer has come close to the kopje, the leopard will be gone, hidden in a crevice.

A leopard's day is spent somewhat as follows: during the hot hours he will lie dozing in a thicket or on a comfortable branch, stirring only if he is hungry and has nothing left to eat from his previous kill. He will consider his hunting program for the evening and will begin to move cautiously and circumspectly to a place where previous experience has taught him he will find a meal. Since a leopard will eat anything from insects to animals larger than himself, his movements have meaning to most inhabitants of the forest and savanna, and they are usually commented on loudly. A leopard on the prowl finds it difficult to move during daylight without causing some kind of commotion. Small, sharp-eyed vervet monkeys will scamper through the trees overhead, chattering and protesting. Baboons, whose eyes are equally keen, and who live in endless war with leopards, set up a furious din of barking. There is a great rustle of leaves and crash of branches as their bodies hurtle through the trees. The large male baboons congregate, sometimes staying on the ground and advancing threateningly on the leopard while the females and babies retreat. In daylight baboons are bold. In a group they know that they are a match for any leopard, and they have been known to surround and kill leopards in bloody fights.

The animal behaviorist Adriaan Kortlandt once set up a stuffed leopard on a forest trail frequented by baboons. The troop quickly spotted it, the males bore down on it in a gang, jumped on it and would have torn it to shreds if Kortlandt had not driven them off.

Nothing like this would happen at night. Then baboons live in deadly fear of leopards. As the sun goes down they congregate quietly in the tops of tall trees where the leopard may not notice them as he pads silently far below. Even if he does, he has a long climb during which his scratching of the bark or shaking of the branches may alert the sleepers. And since baboons weigh only half as much as leopards, they can sleep in—and leap around in—small branches that could not hold a leopard. In a large tree, or even in a fairly small one if it is connected to other trees and hence offers an avenue of escape, a leopard has little chance of catching a baboon, so long as there is enough light for the baboon to see. But in darkness the odds are with the leopard. Having marked the tree that the troop has selected for its night's rest, either by observing them go into it, or by knowing from experience that they use it, or even perhaps by smelling them from the ground, he waits patiently—and there is nothing more patient than a hunting leopard—until they are settled down. Perhaps he has seen them against the sky. Many African trees have rather sparse, feathery leaves, and it may be possible for an animal with night vision as good as a leopard's to pick out dark blobs in the tracery of branches overhead. At any rate, however he may have located his prey, if he can get up the trunk and into the lower branches without too much scratching, he is in business. Sure-footed and as silent as a trickle of sap, he flows upward from limb to smaller limb, testing his weight on each to keep it from trembling. Carefully he considers his route to this or that blob, makes up his mind, inches forward again—and the victim wakes, too late, in its killer's jaws.

Leopards have been so little studied that there is no reliable evidence whatsoever on the frequency with which they take baboons in trees. All that is known is that they are capable of hunting this way, that they do eat a great many baboons and that baboons live in mortal fear of them at night. The probability is, however, that the largest toll is of sick, old or straggling individuals. Where they can, baboons will forego trees entirely in favor of ledges and cracks in rock cliffs and escarpments, where leopards cannot reach them. In such country, the only way a leopard could get a baboon would be to lie in wait for the troop to come by on its way home, or otherwise ambush an individual that strayed too far beyond the group protection afforded by the large males that precede and follow all baboon troops when moving. A leopard is considerably faster than a baboon on the ground, and it is sometimes possible for him to snatch an individual, kill it and make off with it without having to fight the other baboons for possession of his prey. In the event that he is chased off, he can always come back later and claim it.

The lack of good statistical evidence on leopard hunting is by no means limited to the subject of baboons. Nobody really knows what leopards prefer to kill. All that science has succeeded in discovering is that they will eat practically anything, and that there seems to be an extraordinary variety in the habits and preferences of individual leopards. Some live on village dogs. Venn Fey, an astute observer of wildlife, came to know one that apparently doted on bush pigs. Fey was then living in the Kenya Highlands on a farm that bordered a small stand of natural forest. He knew this forest well, liked to walk in it and had cut several paths through it in order to better observe the birds and animals that lived there. The concentration of game in this limited patch of forest, together with the dogs and sheep that belonged to Fey, had attracted leopards in the past, and Fey had been obliged to shoot several of them. Consequently, it was with some concern that he began finding evidence that a new leopard had moved in. To his surprise, the newcomer made no inroads on his livestock, and the game population of the forest appeared to remain stable. He was even more surprised when he discovered the place where the leopard lay up during the day and found it to be only 20 yards away from a similar hide occupied by a bushbuck. Hunter and hunted lived side by side, coming and going for about eight months, with no sign that the leopard ever made the slightest attempt to molest the bushbuck. In an effort to learn what the leopard was eating, Fey began examining its droppings, and he found that they were invariably filled with the stiff black bristles of bush pigs. But bush pigs did not live in this forest; the nearest place they could be found was on a mountainside about two miles away. Whenever this particular leopard wanted a meal, he turned his back on all the juicy targets under his nose and walked two miles for a pig.

Does this mean that the tastes of certain leopards are so refined that they will go to great lengths to satisfy them? Or does it mean that leopards like to hunt in one place and sleep in another? Fey poses the questions but does not know the answers. Nobody does.

Then there is the case of a leopard marooned during a flood on a tiny island, alone with three small antelopes, a hopeless situation from the point of view of the antelopes. Two weeks later the leopard was still there, fat and happy—but so were the three antelopes. A game specialist, Richard Owen, whose job it was to rescue animals from flooded areas, sat down to solve this problem by observation, and he quickly discovered that the leopard was living on fish. It would lie out on a rock and scoop up tilapia as they basked in the warm water near the surface. Again Venn Fey has some questions. Was this leopard a fish-eater from birth? Do many riverine leopards live on fish? Again there are no answers.

A few generalizations are possible about the diet of leopards. They tend to concentrate, sensibly enough, on animals that are in abundant supply in their neighborhood. Given a choice, they prefer species that are big enough to last them for several meals. Like the lion, the leopard has no objection to ripe meat. Flesh begins to putrefy in a few hours in the hot African sun, and within a day or two it is positively stinking. The leopard does not mind. Flesh and maggots go down his throat together, one as nourishing as the other.

Baboons, as noted, are a favorite diet. So are the smaller antelopes, particularly Thomson's gazelle, impala, steenbuck, duiker and klipspringer. The young of some of the larger herbivores are occasionally taken: wildebeest, waterbuck, topi and even young giraffes. On the smaller side the leopard makes out well on cane rats, hares and on the ground-dwelling birds that still abound in large parts of Africa: sandgrouse, francolin, guinea fowl and the like. An odd dietary habit was observed by Venn Fey early one morning when he happened on a large leopard picking his homeward way along a game trail habitually used by buffalo. This animal was delicately turning over the dried pats of buffalo dung that lay in the path and eating the beetles that were congregated underneath.

But whether he is out after beetles or baboons, the leopard is an animal of infinite secretiveness and caution. His ambitions may be bold, but his movements are not. Unnecessary exposure simply is not in him. He slinks. He waits. He drifts from one patch of cover to another—not from necessity but from ingrained habit. As a result, it is likely that he finds and eats a good deal of small game that he almost literally stumbles over as he moves out at dusk to hunt, albeit with bigger things originally on his mind. At night he is about as conspicuous and noisy as a puff of smoke. Many a hunter has sat up over a tethered goat, hoping to get a shot at a marauding leopard, watching and waiting, knowing from a discreet cough uttered an hour before that there is a leopard in the neighborhood. The hunter may have tethered his bait in a piece of open ground. He may have taken the precaution to remove every tuft of grass within yards. The moon may be bright and the bait as prominent as a dancer on an empty ballroom floor. How the leopard gets across the floor unseen is never quite understood. One moment the goat will be placidly feeding; the next it will be down on its back, a leopard's teeth in its throat.

Leopards usually kill with a lethal bite in the throat or neck. They like warm blood, and this they lap up first as long as it flows. They then turn to the abdomen, bite open the skin and, like the lion, remove the intestines, which are carried off and buried. The first parts eaten are the heart, liver and lungs. The feeder then generally turns his attention to the head. He eats the nose, the tongue and sometimes the ears. These hors d'oeuvre out of the way, he gets down to business, starting at the chest and working aft, unlike the lion, who tends to work his way forward.

Having fed himself, the leopard will either drag his prey into deep brush where he will cover it with great skill, or he will put it in a tree. For larger animals that will last him for several feedings, the latter is often the preferred action, and it, more than anything else, testifies to the enormous strength encased in the leopard's slender body. A Thomson's gazelle, weighing only 60 pounds, presents no real problem beyond the awkwardness of dangling hoofs and protruding horns. But what about an impala, which weighs 140 pounds, to say nothing of a 200-pound giraffe calf once found in a tree by a South African hunter? This ungainly bundle, with its huge leg bones and impossible neck, weighing nearly twice as much as its killer, would seem to be beyond the capability of any leopard even to drag, let alone lift off the ground. Yet here it was, safely draped over a branch 12 feet in the air, beyond the leap of hyena or jackal. What makes these feats of the leopard possible is a combination of tremendous leg muscles, a strong neck and a rather short jaw with a viselike bite. Getting a good grip on his prey, the leopard will attempt to claw his way up a tree trunk, carrying the animal with him. If the weight is not too great and the distance to a branch is short, this is no serious problem. But if the animal is a heavy one, the climb takes tremendous exertion and some highly skillful planning. I can think of no way that the young giraffe could have been handled except by being dragged into the tree from above. If, with the neck or a leg in his mouth, the leopard had managed to get as far as a low branch without having to bear the entire weight of his prey while climbing, then, standing on the branch, he may have been able to brace himself, and by degrees hoist his burden upward, changing his grip as needed.

With his prey wedged aloft to his satisfaction, a leopard may not come down from a tree, except to drink, for several days. Or he may leave for a day or two—for reasons known only to himself—and come back later to finish off his kill. Even though it remains unguarded, vultures, those otherwise efficient scavengers, will not touch a leopard's kill in a tree. On the ground, they would be on it in a flash. They will sit ringing a kill, sometimes a hundred or more of them, waiting patiently for the predator to finish. As soon as he moves off they will dive in, grunting and flapping, tearing, snatching, stamping on each other, some of them actually inside the rib cage of the slaughtered animal, covering themselves with blood and offal. Within five or ten minutes they will have eaten everything that has been left and will sit around heavily for a while before taking off to ride the thermals aloft once again in search of their next meal. Vultures are often seen sitting in the next tree to one containing a leopard kill. They may look hopefully at it, but they will not venture to feed on it. Why, I do not know, unless it is because they are fearful that the leopard may be hiding somewhere in the tree. Vultures are large birds and awkward when perched in thick foliage. Perhaps they have learned that they cannot move quickly enough from a branch to avoid a leopard's pounce. There is a nice tale that the bateleur eagle, no mean scavenger himself, keeps vultures away from leopard kills in return for a few bites. But it is no more than a tale. As the writer Jean-Pierre Hallet puts it: "I cannot imagine a leopard making any kind of transaction with a bird, except a rather final one. A leopard doesn't do business with anyone, even another leopard."

A loner to the depths of his being, the leopard never indulges in the social activities one finds in a lion pride. He lives strictly by himself, coming together with a female only for purposes of mating, and then departing. She bears her cubs in solitude and brings them up in solitude. She is an excellent mother, solicitous and resourceful, more conscientious than a lioness and more protective. The only togetherness leopards ever know is when they are growing up as cubs. As soon as they are big enough to get along on their own, they leave.

Because of his stealth and intelligence, his quickness and patience, the leopard, though he hunts alone, enjoys a considerably greater success in his hunting than the lion. Not having a pride to work with, he cannot use the device of the stampede, but must always stalk or wait in ambush. At both he is the lion's superior. And, of course, when he does kill, he has his victim all to himself. Smaller, he needs less food to sustain him. As a result of all these and other factors, there are many more leopards than lions in the world, and they are able to survive over a much wider range. They are found in most parts of Africa, except for true desert areas, and, unlike lions, can and do subsist comfortably in jungles. They even haunt the cold fog-drenched rain forests on the slopes of the Virunga volcanoes on the Congo-Uganda border. This is one of the last strongholds of the mountain gorilla, the largest and most powerful of the apes—male specimens of which exceed 400 pounds. But leopards have learned to hunt gorillas: in one instance, an entire troop of them was nearly exterminated by a single leopard.

Leopards also do remarkably well in close proximity with man. They live in much larger numbers around settled communities than most of the residents ever realize. So good are they at concealment, and so discreet in their movements, that they are almost never seen. However, they take a continuing toll of chickens, goats and sheep, and are absolute death on domestic dogs. In their relations with humans, their activities are a curious mixture of caution and boldness; that uniquely leopardlike blend that gives all their movements the stealth of a creature that trusts nobody or nothing, expects unpleasantness around every corner and is prepared for it, but that at the same time does not hesitate to prowl the streets of villages at night, entering chicken coops, cow pens and even human habitations. In this respect the leopard is far bolder than the lion.

Endless stories emanate from Africa about the leopard's willingness to enter buildings. The following are representative: a government official's daughter goes to her room one evening. Hearing a slight noise, she looks down and sees the tip of a leopard's tail sticking out from under her bed. Keeping her head, she slips quietly out the door and shuts it behind her before calling for help. Another: a man sits eating supper in his bungalow when a leopard suddenly leaps through the open door, skidding wildly across the smooth floor. It recovers in a flash, snatches up a small dog, and is out of the house again before the man can even get up. A third: the owner of a pet leopard finds it in his room instead of chained in the back of the house where it belongs. He seizes a rawhide whip and gives it a severe thrashing until it leaves by the back door. Following it, he finds his leopard sitting chained, just where it is supposed to be—he has thrashed a strange leopard. Probably only the vigor of his assault has kept the leopard from turning on him and killing him.

It is not useful, or even fair, to compare one animal to another, particularly when the comparisons are made in terms of human values. We think of jackals as parasitical and cowardly, lions as courageous and lordly—and as a result we come to the conclusion that one is somehow a more admirable animal than the other. All this is nonsense, of course. Each is tending to his own business, earning his living as he is best adapted to do. Which is "crueler," a muskellunge, a wolf or a wasp? There is no sensible answer to the question, for not one of them is cruel in the sense that humans ordinarily give to the word. Only if one knows better, only if one is imaginative enough to recognize that other living creatures have feelings, only if one kills or injures for one's own amusement, can one be called cruel. By that definition there is only one cruel animal: man.

And yet these labels persist. Hunting animals are generally believed to be ferocious, bloodthirsty, undependable creatures because they kill to live. Deer, on the other hand, are sweet and gentle, with big liquid eyes and timid manners. Doves are soft and meek, the very symbol of peace. But wolves are cruel; eagles are cruel.

It is worth examining the labels for a moment to see how well they really fit. Badly, it turns out. Wolves, except that they hunt, are anything but cruel. They are notably affectionate animals when reared by man. Once their trust has been thoroughly earned, they are devoted and gentle, with the dependability of dogs, except that they are more sensitive, more easily hurt, with finer, sharper feelings than those displayed by the generally thicker-skinned, take-things-as-they-come dog. That liquid-eyed deer, on the other hand, is not as soft-natured as he seems. You may have raised him from babyhood, fed him daily, become used to his trailing around after you. No matter; one day when your back is turned, he may run you through with his antlers. For many years more people have been injured or killed annually in this country by "gentle" horned herbivores than by wolves, mountain lions and bears combined. The dove? Given a chance, he will peck another weaker dove to death. Eagles do not do that.

It is not safe to trust labels, and yet the urge to paste them on the leopard is almost irresistible. His character is so strongly drawn, he is so remote, so cold, so implacable, so self-contained that he stands forth with the hardness and glitter of an emerald. Comparison with the lion is inevitable, and since most of the people who know enough about leopards to have opinions about them are hunters, the lion inevitably comes off better because he is a better animal to hunt. He is "nobler," because he is more predictable, easier to find, easier to kill, less dangerous in close quarters. The leopard is "sneaky."

As quarry for the big-game hunter, Africa provides what is known as the "big five." These are the elephant, the rhinoceros, the Cape buffalo, the lion and the leopard. Opinions are divided as to which deserves first rank as an adversary. Some give it to the elephant because of its huge size, the destructive power of its trunk, tusks and feet, and its intelligence. Others give it to the buffalo because of the murderous effectiveness of its horns and hooves and because of its craftiness and meanness of temper. Many give it to the lion for the qualities described at length in the previous chapter. But, however the big five are rated, the leopard almost invariably comes out at the bottom of the list. One man disagrees: Jean-Pierre Hallet, who has met them all during many years of living in Africa. Hallet puts the leopard at the *top* of the list, and makes a very good case for doing so. His argument starts with the nature of modern big-game hunting. In his book *Animal Kitabu* he dismisses with scathing contempt the farcical experience that the amateur trophy-hunter goes through today when—fortified with trucks and jeeps, high-powered rifles with telescopic sights, game scouts and a battery of professional back-up guns—he sallies forth to bag one of the big animals.

Shooting an elephant under those conditions is about as risky and about as difficult as shooting a silo. A lion presents a smaller target, but if he has been chivvied about by helicopter until he can scarcely run, he is not going to be a very lively one. True, the rules provide that the hunter must get out of his Land Rover and advance on his own two feet a short distance toward his prey. If he only nicks his target, a steadier professional hunter can bring down the animal with a better shot of his own. This hunter might be called the instant sportsman: his real desire is the illusion of having exposed himself to danger—with a photograph to prove it and a trophy for his den. The whole thing would be merely a silly and harmless charade if it did not end with the death of a fine animal. And since what the trophy hunter is seeking is a kill without personal risk and without the expenditure of more than a minimum of effort, the leopard makes a most unsatisfactory quarry. He is seldom seen, difficult to shoot except at night on a baited carcass, and, compared with the other members of the big five, he is disappointingly small. It is very hard to pose for a photograph with one foot triumphantly on a dead leopard in such a way that one appears to have accomplished a brave deed. The leopard's body is too slight; it tends to disappear, even in short grass.

Big-game hunting, it seems to me, must be divided into two categories. There is the arranged sport with the kill almost presented to the hunter's gun, all done as easily and unobtrusively as possible in order to accommodate a visitor who is spending a great deal of money and doesn't have much time, and who, if he doesn't quickly and comfortably get what he came for, will not recommend his safari leader to others. Thus, the safari man has a stake in making hunting easy, and he makes it as easy, as pleasant and as danger-free as he can. Whatever cynical feelings he may have about the whole thing he keeps to himself. Interestingly, few professionals waste time recommending that their clients concentrate on leopards.

Then there is a second kind of hunting, in which one pursues a specific target because one wants it dead. One is not after excitement or a trophy; all one wants is the absence of the animal—a particular animal because it is a menace to domestic stock or even to human beings. One must then track that animal in its own terrain, find it and kill it. It is arduous, time-consuming and often hazardous. This is real hunting. As Hallet makes clear, it is under these conditions that the leopard emerges as the most formidable member of the big five. It is by far the most difficult to find. It is innately the most discreet and suspicious, and probably the most intelligent. It knows man and his ways better than the others, and while it does not fear man, it is respectful of him and can cope with him better. Wounded, it is the most dangerous. Most hunters are agreed that if they have to poke their way into a thicket after a wounded animal, they would prefer that it be a lion rather than a leopard. The problem here is to locate the animal. A lion will sometimes obligingly snarl and growl. If not, it can often be provoked into moving, and the hunter can get off another shot at it, or at least avoid blundering into it. Not so the leopard. Being much smaller, it is more easily concealed, and when wounded and cornered it will remain absolutely still until it considers that the advantage of an attack is in its favor —that is, until it can spring at close range from the side or rear. It is extraordinarily quick and agile, and a man jumped by a leopard in thick brush has little chance of survival. Unlike the lion, which may sometimes merely maul a hunter before running off, a leopard will invariably try to kill him. As Stevenson-Hamilton puts it: "He may be relied upon always to charge home: the possibility of his losing heart and stopping or swerving at the last moment is so slight as to be not worth reckoning on." He should know. As a trapper and hunter in predator-control programs in South Africa, he killed leopards by the score, and had a professional's respect for them. This kept him out of trouble, something that Hallet was once unable to avoid.

Hallet's brush with a leopard was due to no carelessness of his own. He was on a routine safari in the eastern Congo, bringing up the rear in a line of 16 Africans who were working their way slowly along an overgrown forest trail. Suddenly a porter at the head of the line noticed a leopard on a branch almost over his head. Instead of standing his ground, the man uttered a panicky scream and tried to run. Instantly the leopard jumped on him. The other men scattered, leaving Hallet to run forward and deal with this emergency as best he could.

Hallet is a big and agile man, weighing about 250 pounds. But he has only one hand, having lost the other some years ago in an accident. Unarmed, he could not shoot or stab the leopard, which was savaging the man, so he threw himself on its back, getting a full nelson on it, gripping the stump of his right arm with his left hand. At the same time with his legs he secured a good scissors grip lower down to keep himself from being disemboweled by the animal's flailing hind claws. Glued in this manner to the back of the leopard, and momentarily secure, Hallet exerted all his strength to force its head forward and break its neck, or, failing that, to dislocate its shoulders. But it was much stronger than he had expected. It reacted like a coiled spring, choking and snarling, thrashing and twisting and, although it was less than half of Hallet's weight, repeatedly rolling him over and over in the bushes.

This extraordinary struggle went on for nearly 20 minutes while Hallet yelled to the other porters for help. But they were too frightened to approach, and most of them were watching from the trees as Hallet hung on, wondering whether his strength or the leopard's would give out first. Finally one of the men threw him a large knife. Hallet risked loosening his full nelson long enough to grab the knife, and after a couple of desperate thrusts at his twisting adversary, in which he nearly stabbed himself, he succeeded in sinking the knife in the leopard's chest. When the battle was over, Hallet was so exhausted that he could scarcely stand. His arms and legs were covered with blood, but this was from hundreds of scratches and gashes from the thorn bushes that he had been tossed around in. The leopard had not touched him.

Examination of the carcass proved it to be a 120-pound male in fine condition. Hallet was baffled by its un-leopardlike attack in broad daylight and with other adult humans about. He assumed that it must have been extremely hungry. However, it may also be that it was responding to the very strong urge, present in many hunting animals, to pursue something that runs away. As Hallet himself points out, when Pygmies encounter leopards in the forest, they always stand their ground and shout loudly to the leopards to go away. According to him, they do.

A wounded animal is quite another matter. A conscientious hunter will, whenever possible, try to make sure that the lion or leopard he has shot is dead. This is not only for humane reasons, but for safety. By the simple fact of being wounded, it has become dangerous and may attack. At worst, it may escape to live on as a cripple and become a man-eater because of its inability to catch wild game. This is where the principal danger in hunting big cats arises: in finishing them off. A wounded animal will often conceal itself in a thicket, and it is up to the hunter somehow to get it out and shoot it, or go in after it. With experience and caution, and particularly with dogs to help, this can be done. Alone, it is a deadly game. It becomes even more deadly if the quarry has been only slightly injured and takes it into its head to stalk and kill the hunter.

That is what happened to Carl Akeley, the famous American naturalist and collector who procured and mounted many of the specimens now in the Museum of Natural History in New York. Akeley was on a collecting expedition in the semi-desert country of Somalia, and having shot a warthog, whose head he wanted for the Museum, he came back later in the afternoon to pick it up. Finding it gone, he poked around for a while. By this time dusk was gathering, and when he saw a movement behind a bush, he foolishly took a quick shot without checking to make sure what he was shooting at. An explosion of coughs told him that he had inadvertently put a bullet into a leopard. In near darkness, Akeley discreetly decided to leave things as they were, and return the next morning to try to track it and kill it. He backed off, dropping down into a dry stream bed and climbing up the other side to a small island formed by a sharp bend in the stream. As he got to the top he looked back, and to his dismay saw the leopard coming through the stream bed after him. He took several more quick shots at it, finally stopping it with another hit. He was congratulating himself for having gotten out of a messy situation more easily than he deserved when there was another salvo of snarling coughs from the stream bed, and the leopard came at him again. He shot again. Click! His rifle was empty.

All this time he had been holding a single extra cartridge in his hand. In a flash of panic he realized that his only chance lay in finding the time to get the bullet into his gun. As the leopard scrambled up the bank, Akeley hurled himself down the other side and ran off along the bed of the stream, fumbling at his rifle as he ran. He finally got the bullet in, wheeled to shoot—but he was too late. The account that follows is from his book, *Lions, Gorillas and Their Neighbors*.

"Immediately I was face to face with the leopard in mid-air. My trusty rifle was knocked flying from my hands and in my arms was the leopard—eighty pounds of furious bloodthirsty cat. I knew she intended to sink her teeth into my throat and hold me tight in the grip of her jaws and fore-paws while with her hind paws she dug out my stomach—for this practice is the pleasant way of leopards. But unexpectedly enough and most happi-ly for me, she missed her aim. Instead of clutching my throat she struck me high in the chest and caught my upper right arm in her mouth. Thus not only was my throat saved but her hind legs were left hanging clear where she could not reach my stomach.

"With my left arm I seized her throat and tried to wrench my right arm free, but this I could do only little by little. When I got grip enough on her throat to loosen her hold just a bit, she would seize and set her jaws again in my arm an inch or two further down. In this way, I drew the full length of my arm inch by inch through her slavering poisonous mouth. During all this time I was not conscious of any pain whatsoever but only of the sound of the crushing of tense muscles and the choking, snarl-ing grunts of the infuriated beast. As I pushed her jaws farther and farther down my arm, I bent over and finally, when my arm was almost free, I fell to the ground—the leopard underneath me. My right hand was now in her mouth, my left hand clutched her throat, my knees were on her chest, my elbows in her armpits which spread her front legs so far apart that her frantic clawing did nothing more than tear my shirt. Here we both struggled for life, man and beast. We were both determined to die hard. The leopard writhed and twisted her body in an effort to get hold of the ground and turn herself over, but the loose shifting sand offered her no hold or purchase. . . .

"Now during all this time, my original state of abject, helpless terror had changed utterly into one of complete physical anesthesia and of the greatest mental activity. All dread of death had vanished and the only sense of physical hurt I· had at all was toward the end, when with my hand shoved down her throat, my thumb was pinched by the animal's mo-lars. . . .I continued to shove my right hand down her throat so far and so hard that she could not close her jaws. With my other hand I gripped her throat in a strangle hold. Then I surged down hard upon her with my knees, putting all the power in them I could muster. To my surprise I felt a rib break. I began to feel sure of myself. I did it again. Another rib cracked. Then I felt her relax, a sort of easing up and letting go, though she continued to struggle. Now at the same time I felt myself weakening in like manner. I had done my utmost. Soon it would become a question as to which one would give up first. But I resummoned my failing strength and held on to the big cat and thrust my knees down on her chest again. Little by little her struggling ceased. The fight was finished. *My strength had outlasted hers.*"

Dreadfully mauled, Akeley staggered back to camp, where his companions pumped so much antiseptic solution into his wounds that "an extra shot in one gash drove it out of another." He was put to bed and the body of the leopard brought in to show him. Examining it later, he discovered that his first shot had broken its right hind foot. That had spoiled its aim when it first jumped on him, and that alone had saved his life.

Both Hallet and Akeley were unbelievably lucky to have emerged alive from their respective hand-to-hand encounters. One had the advantage of surprise, the other was dealing with an adversary handicapped by a broken foot. But despite these advantages, both were nearly overborne by animals whose sheer strength and ferocity they had underestimated. This is easy to do, for leopards are deceptively small. Males run from 100 to 180 pounds in weight, females 20 to 30 pounds less. They stand about two feet high at the shoulder; from nose to tail tip they average seven feet.

The leopard is somewhat differently proportioned than the lion. It is not as short-coupled or as deep-chested. Its head is rounder and a trifle smaller for its size, its nose less prominent. Its movements are entirely different. There is something almost ponderous in a lion's walk, particularly that of a mature male, who will bring his hind leg forward rather stiffly and plant it with a visible shifting of body weight. This is a big animal moving. Things happen with a reasonable slowness, and they can be seen happening, as in the awkward-graceful stride of a walking race horse. There is none of that in the leopard. He is all bunched muscle, under constant tension. He glides and crouches, his belly low, his chin lower. He is of a single piece, like quicksilver, changing shape and flowing—with the whole mechanism being integrated with such incomparable smoothness that one is never conscious of the contribution of any part to the movement of the whole.

His appearance matches his actions. Together they make up one of the most beautiful animals in the world. His coat is softer and silkier than the lion's, being a yellowish tawny on the back, shading to white on the belly. Some animals have a light rufous coat. But all of them, whatever the background tint, are prominently marked with black spots. These occur all over the body, on the toes, tail, except on the inner sides of the ears. Around the head the spots are small and numerous—single black dots.

But elsewhere they are larger, particularly on the back and flanks, where they occur in characteristic clusters, or rosettes. Thus, most of a leopard's most prominent "spots" actually consist of circular groups of four or five smaller spots that look very much like the pawprints of an animal.

The eyes are yellowish green, a more remote and glacial color than the warm golden amber of a lion's eye, and adding just one more note to the overall appearance of implacability that the leopard wears, even in repose. This is enhanced by a slight but satanic slant in the positioning of the eye.

The tail of a leopard is somewhat longer for its size than a lion's; a seven-foot specimen will often have as much as three feet of its length represented by tail. But size is only the beginning of the differences between the appendages. The lion has a rather stiff tail. It tapers slightly from its base to the tuft at its end and is not capable of sharp turns or twists. Its natural position, when its owner is standing or walking, is to extend to the rear, falling gradually into a gentle curve that rises slightly again at the tip. This curve can be tightened somewhat, almost into a circle in some individuals, but generally it seems to have not much more flexibility than the tail of a long-tailed dog, a setter or greyhound. One gets the feeling, watching a walking lion, that it would have to depress its tail deliberately in order to have it touch the ground; otherwise it would remain in that shallow springy curve. A lion twitches its tail and often uses it for caresses but otherwise does not do much with it.

The tail of a leopard dangles like a velvet rope. So limp is it, and so long, that it would drag on the ground if the latter half of it were not held up. It tapers almost not at all, has no tuft at the end, and is under very precise muscular control from root to tip. All sorts of passing fancies ripple through it. There may be a couple of soft wayward kinks in it, or it may be held out as rigid as a bar. It is endlessly expressive. When its owner is in a tree, it hangs straight down, apparently without a spark of life in it. But, as one watches, an inch or two may curl ever so slightly to reflect a mood as fleeting as the shadow of a cloud passing over a meadow, an unconscious understatement of incomparable elegance.

Leopards vary greatly in size and coloring, so much so that taxonomists have split them into innumerable races. This is a dull subject, open to endless argument, and is not a fit topic for discussion here. It is only worth noting that leopards inhabiting very dry hot country tend—in common with many other kinds of animals—to be light in color and light in weight. These are adaptive characteristics. Light color reflects sunlight and heat, and thus keeps the animal cooler than if it had a dark coat, which would absorb heat. Also a slender rangy build presents to the air more skin surface per unit of body weight than a chunky build, and is more efficient in getting rid of body heat. By contrast, leopards that live in forests and mountains, where it is cooler, are darker and more heavily built. A curious trait in leopards is melanism, the occasional appearance of an all-black individual. As might be expected, this trait is much more common among mountain than among semi-desert populations.

Although black leopards may look black, there are degrees of blackness. Some of them, if looked at in the right light, display the same unexpected deep reddish glint that may be detected in the hair of a black-haired girl seen in bright sunlight. Under such circumstances the leopard's darker rosettes can be seen as a blacker black.

In his regular colors the leopard is much sought after. His spectacular markings have brought him into high fashion in Europe and the United States as a source of fur coats, hats and handbags. A leopard coat is undeniably beautiful, but it wears badly, does not keep out the cold particularly well and, considering the cost today, is a poor bargain. Demand in western fashion centers has given rise to a large poaching industry, mostly in Ethiopia, Somalia and Kenya—from which an estimated 50,000 leopard skins are illegally shipped each year. It is a wretched traffic. The poacher takes most of the risks and gets the least money—and usually all of the blame. He is paid only two or three dollars per skin for his labors, and if he is caught he is sent to jail. The skins pass through various hands, arriving in New York worth several hundred dollars apiece. It takes up to seven skins to make one coat, and by the time these have been matched and made up into a garment, the price charged by a fashionable New York furrier may run as high as $20,000.

From any point of view poaching is barbarous, since it is usually accomplished with snares, traps or poison—all of which mean a slow death for the victim. His best hope is to be found and quickly eaten by another predator; otherwise he may linger on for days, slowly dying of thirst in the broiling sun. While the poacher fills the role of supplier in the leopard skin traffic, he is the least to blame. He leads a hard life with almost no opportunity of making money, and the temptation to poach is very strong. The real villain is the consumer, for if the demand for leopard skins were to fall off, the poachers would stop poaching. If this book has any success in persuading any of its readers not to buy leopard coats or to boycott a store that sells these articles, its authors will feel repaid for their work.

There is a side effect to poaching that works a great hardship on the African villager. Leopards are an important factor in controlling the populations of such species as bush pigs and baboons, and if the leopards are completely exterminated from an area, the pigs and baboons will rapidly increase in numbers. The baboons raid village gardens during the day, the pigs by night, and between them they have been known to starve out entire communities. As Guy Muldoon, a professional game-control man from Nyasaland, writes: "Villagers and baboons are actually in a state of war from one planting to the next and the daily skirmishes can be counted not by the hundred but by the thousand. For the Africans it is an exhausting and heartbreaking ordeal. . . . I have traveled through the territory extensively, and it has been no uncommon experience to find village after village empty, the grass and weeds growing right up to the doors of the huts, because the inhabitants have all been compelled to take up their abode in the nearby fields and gardens to try to keep the baboons from getting at their crops."

Muldoon goes on to point out that in many places the villagers build special shacks on stilts or in trees, not only to survey the fields better, but also for protection at night from lions, leopards and hyenas. And it is the presence of these animals—notably the leopards—that puts a man like Muldoon in a quandary. For leopards do not always feed on baboons. Like lions, they may be driven by age or injury to become man-eaters. As a consequence, Muldoon, who may have been trying to decimate the baboons in a particular area, has also been called upon to kill a leopard—the baboon's enemy—because it has turned its attentions to human beings.

As a man-killer, the leopard is efficiency incarnate—far worse than the lion. Always circumspect, he seldom works in daylight, and if he does, his victim is usually a child that has strayed from home, or a woman working alone in a field. Men are seldom, if ever, attacked during the day, but at night all such distinctions vanish. In a village being preyed on by a man-eater everyone is in danger after dark, even inside houses. The man-eater's presence may not be recognized at first. If a woman is killed quickly and quietly in a remote garden patch, and if the remains of her body are not accidentally found, it may take another death or two before the community becomes aware of the curse that has stricken it. This realization can be utterly demoralizing. Women will become terrified of moving out into their gardens, children will be kept cooped up at home. Nobody will show his face after sundown. As a result, the leopard will become more and more ag-

(continued on page 121)

Right front pawprint of leopard

THE LEOPARD

Rounder-headed than the lion, the leopard is even more heavily muscled for his size, with a powerful neck and a viselike jaw. He has small, rounded ears and eyes of an icy greenish hue, and his face is peppered with small spots that gradually become larger farther back on his body and turn into characteristic clusters. He has a luxuriant crop of whiskers, which are important to him as organs of touch and are used for the precise location of twigs and leaves as he pursues his stealthy way of stalk and pounce—usually in the dark. Much of the leopard's time is spent in trees, and since many of these are bristling with large thorns, his whiskers and eyebrow hairs are also useful in helping him avoid them. In fact, such is his all-round dexterity in trees that thorns do not really hinder him at all. Many an observer has watched a leopard daintily nip off a thorn here and another there so that he can comfortably settle himself on a branch. A leopard's eyes are like those of other big cats in having round pupils that retain their roundness even when shrunk to pinpoint size in bright light, as in this picture. The smaller cats belong to a different genus; they have eyes that narrow to vertical slits.

On the ground the leopard can move with tremendous agility over a short distance, proceeding with great soft-footed bounds. The animal pictured here is a captive taken by John Dominis out into the dry thorn bush country of Botswana to hunt baboons. These photographs show him moving into high gear as he spots a baboon that immediately climbs a tree to get away. The sequence on the following two pages shows what happened next. In the first picture the leopard swarms up the tree while the baboon anxiously jumps about in the upper branches. Realizing that the tree is too small for safety, the baboon leaps to the ground and runs off, while the leopard launches himself like a projectile in pursuit. This particular baboon had just enough of a head start to reach some larger trees where the leopard was unable to catch it. Another baboon, however (*pages 114-115*), was not so lucky. John Dominis' extraordinary photograph was taken at the very instant at which the baboon, realizing it could not outrun the leopard, whirled to face its nemesis.

The leopard kills with a crunching bite in the throat or neck of his victim. His jaw is relatively short, which gives him immense leverage, and his jaw muscles are very large, which is one of the reasons his face is as round as it is. Having killed, the leopard often drags his victim into a tree to keep it secure from other predators. The picture on the next page shows a leopard with a freshly killed springbok. Though these animals weigh up to 80 pounds each, a leopard can easily hoist one into the trees. Each supplies three or four days' food. Toward the end of this time, the remaining meat is thoroughly rotten, but leopards finish it off anyway, seeming to enjoy it as much as meat they have just killed.

On the prowl a leopard moves with infinite
caution, his head low. Like the lion, he is a
grabber of prey that is sometimes larger
and heavier than he is. As a result, his neck
and shoulder muscles are exceptionally well
developed, as is clearly shown in this
picture of a stalking leopard. Also shown
are the characteristic "leopard's spots";
each "spot" is actually a cluster of four or
five smaller spots, appearing almost like
pawprints on the animal's body.

gressive, as the opportunity for picking off easy victims dwindles. It is then that a villager may waken some night to a persistent scratching at the thatch of his hut and realize that there is a leopard outside trying to get in. If he is bold, and if he happens to have a club or spear handy, he may succeed in driving it off. But if he is a heavy sleeper, or if he is away and the hut is occupied only by his wife or children, the leopard may claim another victim. And she may scream and scream, but nobody will dare come from the other huts to help. This piracy may go on for months, and the villagers, if they are not hunters by tradition, will be helpless.

Occasionally a man-eating leopard will stop its depredations as mysteriously as it started them. Someone may have succeeded in wounding it; there is a record of a leopard that was badly scalded and scared away by a pot of hot soup thrown on it by a desperate householder. Or it may simply have decided to move elsewhere. It could even die—of old age or injuries—its last meal possibly a human one.

Usually when a man-eater is discovered operating in a certain neighborhood the word gets around very quickly. A plea for help will go out, and somebody like Muldoon, who knows the country, who knows the people and who knows leopards, will be asked to kill it. During his years in Nyasaland Muldoon responded to a number of such requests and managed to free several communities from man-eating leopards. Sometimes he failed. Assessing his experiences, he came to the same conclusion that virtually every leopard hunter has come to: the best way to get the animal is to sit over its kill, hoping that it will return to it.

Knowing this, he once had the difficult job of persuading the inhabitants of a remote country village near Kota Kota on the eastern side of Lake Nyasa to let him sit up over the body of a 13-year-old boy who had been taken in a reed bed by a river the previous evening. He had never sat over a human kill before and did not relish the idea. Nor did the village headman when Muldoon explained what he proposed to do.

"'Look how the leopard has already eaten this child,' the headman said. 'Is that not bad enough? How can we do such a thing as to leave it to be completely eaten?' "

These were hard questions, and harder yet when put by the boy's father. But Muldoon insisted, promising that the leopard would not touch the boy again, and pointing out that as long as it remained free it would kill others. Finally the father consented, and Muldoon put the villagers to work digging a six-and-a-half-foot pit for him to hide in. Over this they placed a bamboo roof covered with sod. The end of the roof was raised slightly, leaving a narrow slit so that Muldoon, standing inside, could look out at the corpse of the boy lying on the ground directly in front of him. Just before dark he and his game scout, Akin, got in the pit. They sent the villagers home, and took turns standing watch, a half hour at a time, through the slit.

For two hours nothing happened. Then there came the faint cough by which leopards so often announce their presence in a locality. This was followed by a long silence during which Muldoon and Akin stood side by side in the dark, not daring to move or whisper. Suddenly Akin touched his shoulder. He looked up and there was a black shadow standing almost over him, so close that if he had pushed his rifle fully out of the slit he could have touched it. He was afraid to bring it back to his shoulder to shoot, for fear that he might make a noise, so, holding it in both hands about six inches from his shoulder, he aimed it upward at the leopard's chest and pulled the trigger. The recoil slammed him against Akin and the flash momentarily blinded him, but when he was able to see again, he could make out the leopard squirming on the ground. A few more shots finished it off, and the villagers came running. After much congratulating all around, the carcass was carried back to the village. There an old woman shook him earnestly by the hand, saying: "You must come and live here. Then things like this will never happen again."

It is hard for people living in civilized communities to comprehend the force of terror and despair that assails a group of defenseless villagers when a man-eater moves in on them. It is not unlike a disease epidemic for which no known antitoxin exists. The unearthly arrival of an unstoppable and deadly presence, capricious in its choice, often unseen by any but its victims, has convinced many Africans that man-killers are supernatural beings who inhabit the bodies of leopards. This conviction can lead to a kind of fatalism that reduces effective resistance to the leopard to near zero. As a result, if no deliverer in the form of a white hunter comes along, the leopard's activities can continue indefinitely. He will kill when he needs to, sometimes humans, sometimes dogs or goats, roaming from village to village within a radius of a few miles—but always, no matter how often he kills, acting with the greatest caution. That is what makes such a formidable adversary of the leopard. He leaves nothing to chance. Having killed and eaten a hundred goats in his lifetime and knowing that goats are weak, defenseless creatures, he will approach the hundred-and-first as if it were a time bomb. Who may be watching, what the trap may be, the leopard does not know. But he is endlessly suspicious. Many a hunter has waited over a tethered goat, and has almost burst from tension while a leopard has conducted a careful reconnaissance of more than an hour—just to leap on something it *knows* cannot harm it. This is a puzzling matter. Caution is to be expected from leopards that have been shot at or have escaped from traps. But all leopards seem cautious when stalking, no matter how bold they may be in deciding what to stalk or where to go after it. When they learn something of man's ability to strike back, they lose none of their boldness of design, but their caution in execution only increases.

It should be remembered that a man-eater is probably a cautious animal to begin with, one that has already had some experience with humans, and whose man-eating habit may even have been the result of a man-inflicted wound that has made it difficult for it to hunt ordinary prey. Even so, the extent to which such an animal will go to avoid detection while it is hunting is extraordinary. The most elusive leopard, and probably the most notorious man-killer of all time, was not an African but an Indian one. It lived in Garhwal in the foothills of the Himalayas, and got its name, Man-eater of Rudraprayag, from the hill village around which its activities were centered. It was killed by the celebrated hunter of man-eating tigers, Jim Corbett, on May 2, 1926. Its first recorded victim was taken on June 9, 1918. During the eight years of its activity it killed 125 human beings for certain. Most of these were pilgrims and itinerant holy men, news of whose deaths kept the Indian press in a furor, and hence built up the leopard's notoriety. (Another animal, living in a more remote area, and preying on obscure hill tribesmen, killed more than 400 people.)

How many other humans should be added to the toll of the Rudraprayag leopard cannot be accurately estimated because of the local method of recording. When a kill by the man-eater was reported, the body was examined by an official to make sure that the case was not one of human murder being blamed on a leopard. If it passed that test, it was entered against the account of the leopard. But in cases where bodies were not recovered (and they often were not because the leopard sometimes dragged them for considerable distances before eating them) the leopard got no credit. Nor did he for people he mauled severely who later died from their wounds, or for others who simply disappeared. Corbett cautiously made no estimate of the numbers that might have been added to the Rudraprayag man-eater's total of 125, but it could have been several score more.

During the years of his operations, that one leopard changed the living habits of every man, woman and child in a district of about 500 square miles. He worked only at night, and as a result, daily activities went on as usual, but as soon as darkness fell, everyone—some 50,000 people—made sure to be safely at home with doors and windows bolted. Meanwhile the leopard went his rounds, padding silently from village to village, killing a sheep here, a dog there, breaking into a house in another place and carrying off its human occupant. Once he came through a window without dislodging a large brass vase that stood in his way, went through a room in which a man was sleeping, killed a sick woman lying between two friends in an inner room, and was not detected until, trying to drag the woman out through the window again, he knocked the vase over. Another time he broke into a room in which 40 goats were penned, passed through this terrified mob and carried off the goat boy who was sleeping in the corner. This selectivity was totally unnerving. Few houses failed to show the scratch marks of the leopard's claws on their doors or window shutters. In all, 77 mountain hamlets lost at least one human victim, and one of them, a place named Chopra, lost six.

Because of his fame as a tiger hunter, Corbett was persuaded to take on the Rudraprayag leopard. He spent several months at it, sometimes with a friend, sometimes alone. This was Kipling country he was operating in— snuggled up against the western end of Nepal. It was an endless tumble of steep rugged hills, dotted with tiny villages and patches of farm. Where the land was not cultivated it was heavily forested. Perpendicular gorges with foaming little icy rivers plunged downward to the Ganges. Narrow roads that had never known a wheel but had been marked for centuries by the footprints of pilgrims wound upward through the hills. Up and beyond lay the silent white snows of Himalayan peaks—a stunningly wild and beautiful world that no one has described better than Corbett himself in his book, *Man-Eaters of India*.

It was a hard place to find and kill a wily leopard. The first thing Corbett realized was that he could cut the man-eater's area in half by keeping it to one side or another of a river that ran through the center of its territory. Two bridges crossed this river; Corbett plugged one with thorn bushes and for 20 nights watched at the other, waiting for the leopard to appear. His vantage point was a rickety wooden platform jutting over the torrent. Here he lay, his gun ready, the Himalayan winds howling down the gorge and almost blowing him from his perch and an army of tiny biting ants tormenting him. During all that time nothing crossed the bridge but a single jackal. The leopard, meanwhile, was making good use of its time with the villagers and their stock on the opposite side. So Corbett blocked up the second bridge and moved over to where the action was.

Whenever an animal or a human was killed—and Corbett had opportunities with both—he would plan an ambush over the corpse. When these failed, he bought goats and sat up over them. He got little sleep and less food. On one occasion he walked up and down hill for 18 miles in the hope of catching the leopard returning to the body of a boy it had killed. When he got there the leopard had fed itself and gone.

Thanks to a lifetime of tracking and shooting in the Indian hills, and to an uncanny knowledge of animals, he was able to learn a good deal about his quarry. He could recognize its pug marks instantly, and knew them for the prints of an elderly animal of exceptional size, strong despite its years. Once it carried a heavy human corpse for two miles up a steep brush-choked mountainside and then two miles down the other side before stopping to eat it. Once or twice Corbett saw it, once he got a shot at it, several times it stalked and nearly got him. His accounts of his vigils are unforgettable. He would settle himself in a tree over a victim, or over a live goat staked in full view a few yards away. He would wait. The afternoon shadows would draw in, and across the valley the icy peaks would glow pink for a few glorious minutes. As the dark came an immense silence would settle down, punctuated only by an occasional bleat from his goat. Sometimes the leopard came. Once it announced its presence accidentally with a pine cone that bounced down the hillside past his feet. On other occasions the bark of a small deer or the sudden alertness of the goat would signal its arrival. But always some unforeseen accident frustrated the hunter. Corbett had excellent night vision and could see to shoot by starlight, to say nothing of moonlight. But a couple of times heavy clouds obliterated both just before the leopard arrived. Once a heavy rain washed out his hopes. Another time, though he had built a thorn hedge around his bait to ensure the leopard's approaching from a certain direction, the animal crossed him up by perversely clawing its way through the hedge from behind. It was infernally clever. Twice it twitched the bait from the jaws of big traps without setting them off. Once a trap snapped shut on a tiny patch of skin and a few hairs, but the leopard got away. Once it survived a meal of flesh heavily laced with cyanide.

Knowing that it had fairly tender pads and preferred to walk on the local paths rather than through the brush, Corbett finally decided to wait it out on a particular road that he knew the leopard often traveled. For 11 nights he sat in a small tree waiting, with a goat tethered in the middle of the road, before the leopard came. He put one bullet into it but had to wait until daylight before he dared descend the tree and track it to where it had crawled and died—a few yards away among some rocks. As he had guessed, it was an old animal with several bullet wounds, a broken tooth, and minus part of a toe and one claw.

Some sense of the profound relief that the district felt on learning the news that its nemesis was dead may be found in a moving epilogue to Corbett's account of the Rudraprayag man-eater. Years later, during World War II, he was invited to a garden party to help entertain some wounded Indian soldiers. One young man was so severely injured that he could scarcely move from the low chair he had been placed in. But, on hearing who Corbett was, he slid himself somehow to the ground and put his head on Corbett's feet, explaining that he was a Garwhali, and as a little boy had been prevented from going to see the dead leopard on the day that Corbett killed it because his father had been too weak to carry him the long distance through the hills. "'And now, Sahib,'" he said to Corbett, "'I will go back to my home with great joy in my heart, for I shall be able to tell my father that with my own eyes I have seen you, and maybe, if I can get anyone to carry me to the *Mela* [celebration] that is annually held at Rudraprayag to commemorate the death of the man-eater, I shall tell all the people I meet there that I have seen and had speech with you.'"

If these grisly stories are not enough to establish Jean-Pierre Hallet's claim that the leopard deserves number one spot on the list of the big five, others could be told; the literature is full of them. And, by emphasizing the deadly skills and strength of the leopard as an adversary of man, the stories always seem to carry the same implied message: the leopard is a "bad" animal. Of course he is not, a point that Corbett himself made very clear. When he stood at last over the body of the Rudraprayag man-eater, he saw only an old leopard: "the best-hated and most-feared animal in all India, whose only crime—not against the laws of nature, but against the laws of man—was that he had shed human blood, with no object of terrorizing man, but only in order that he might live."

THE CHEETAH

One of the most beautiful and distinctive game reserves in all Africa is the Masai Amboseli, which lies in southern Kenya, almost under the shadow of Mt. Kilimanjaro. It is also one of the most fragile. Its heart is a slowly shrinking swamp, an oasis of green in a countryside that is predominantly dry, dusty and thorny. One approach to the park is along the edge of a large alkali flat that would surely become a lake if a few wet seasons were to occur back to back, and just as surely once was a lake before the drying-up process became acute. Now, however, it is a gray, crusty waste, sometimes with an inch of water on it, more often pocked with the hoofprints of innumerable cattle which belong to Masai tribesmen living in the area, and which are constantly invading the precincts of the reserve itself. So, as Amboseli dries up, it is also being nibbled away at the edges. But as it dies its beauty endures. The shadows from majestic trees still dapple the backs of elephant and rhino. The snows of Kilimanjaro's summit glow with a violet light at dawn. And the springs that nourish the swamp still produce bright stands of reed around little pools where marsh birds with preposterously long toes scamper about on the floating lily pads, stepping quickly from one tiny green raft to another before it can sink beneath them.

The oasis also attracts antelopes: impala and duiker and the long-necked gerenuk are all found in Amboseli, along with the ubiquitous Thomson's gazelle. During the heat of the day they stand motionless in the shaded thickets while the mirages boil and dance on the horizon. But if one is out early, one will find them out too, grazing among the brownish clumps of grass. And it was there one morning that I saw two heads among the grass clumps. I thought at first that they were hyenas lying down to watch the impala, each head hidden behind its clump. But these heads were too small for hyenas. As I came closer, their owners got up—a pair of lithe, long-legged hunters that gave the impression of being a cross between leopard and greyhound. They were cheetahs, the first I had ever seen.

Together they walked off. Elegant, unhurried, they moved in unison almost like a pair of dancers, an illusion that was strengthened by the way they turned their heads together to look back—not so much to look at me as simply to look around. Cheetahs do not seem to look at people. In them there is none of the intense, cold, concentrated stare of the leopard or the sleepy disinterest of the lion. Cheetahs are alert, but to a music of their own. They look past you; their eyes are on other things, on distant animals that they might catch and kill.

Almost anybody who has observed a cheetah will agree that he is handsome. But with this agreement often go some reservations: his head seems too small for his body; he is all knees and legs; he is hump-necked; he is sway-backed; he is too pinched at the waist. For me none of these things matter. I think the cheetah is the most beautiful animal I have ever seen. And I could not get enough of looking at that first pair. I was filled with an intense joy just from watching them, and every cheetah I have seen since has given me the same feeling.

Some people respond to thoroughbred horses, or to this or that breed of dog. I respond to cheetahs. The small head, set low, looks just right to me. The deep chest and vanishing waist are of an aching perfection, hung on those slender, swinging, springing legs. The cheetah's walk is unmistakable—deliberate, easy, and not in the least menacing. The implacable heavy pace of a lion and the muscular skulk of the leopard both bring a shiver. But the cheetah steps delicately and sedately. He may give pause to an antelope—indeed he does—but not to man. He gives the impression of being an aristocratic, gentle animal, contained within himself. But also contained within him is something else, something that gives meaning and unity to every part of his unusually proportioned body. That something is speed; the cheetah is the fastest mammal in the world.

Anyone who has examined the lion and the leopard and has found them to be so different in habits and personality will be astonished to find that there could be a third large cat in Africa that is totally different again. Cheetahs share the savanna with lions and leopards, and they share with them the smaller antelopes, but they have their own way of catching them. They are neither true stalkers nor do they lie in ambush. They are coursers. They hunt by sight and in daylight. They often resort to a preliminary stalk in order to come within a hundred yards or so of their prey. Then they can, by putting on a burst of super speed, overhaul it and knock it down. Estimates of the cheetah's top speed run all the way from 45 to 75 miles an hour. Now that vehicles with speedometers are common in the

game parks, the estimates begin to have some validity; hitherto they were
mere guesses. It appears that a full-grown animal in good condition can
reach 60 miles an hour. But he is a sprinter; he can run flat out for only
15 or 20 seconds. At this speed, of course, he will cover a quarter of a mile
in that time. And if he gets a good jump on his prey he will probably
catch it. Ranging alongside, he usually will try to knock it off stride by hitting it in the hind legs or flanks with his own forelegs thrust out stiffly.
This kind of a blow is enough to send a small antelope staggering; the cheetah will then pounce on it and kill it with a bite in the throat.

Watching a cheetah really stretch out is a thrilling sight. In a few
jumps he is traveling at top speed. He does not go straight and level like a
galloping horse. That is because a horse has a stiff backbone and gets all
its drive from its legs. As any rider knows, the faster a horse runs, the
smoother the ride. The cheetah's backbone, by contrast, is extremely supple. It coils and uncoils like a spring, and thus there is an up-and-down
undulation to his movement as he proceeds with great 25-foot bounds.

Some interesting experiments have been made with tame cheetahs on
dog tracks. In one instance, with the mechanical rabbit set for greyhound
speed, the cheetahs caught it and demolished it in a few jumps. So the rabbit speed was greatly increased; whereupon the cheetahs, realizing that
they could not catch the rabbit, refused to run at all. On another occasion
they were released with some greyhounds. Seeing them disappear down
the track, the cheetahs took out after them, caught up with ridiculous
ease and leaped right over them. No one yet, however, has had any success in getting cheetahs to compete with cheetahs. They apparently have
no interest in trying to outrun each other.

How the cheetah evolved from the ancestral cats is not well known, for
the fossil evidence is negligible. But we can speculate that he has followed
a coursing life for a long time because he is so highly specialized today. He
is the most uncatlike of all the cats. Except for the fact that he is not particularly gregarious, he is the most like a dog, an animal designed for
running. Every part of his body shows the effects of evolutionary shaping—
and in some cases sacrificing—for speed. Like a racing yacht, all surplus
weight has been removed. Although the cheetah is about as big as the average leopard, standing taller at the shoulder, and just as long from nose to
tail tip, he is much more slender. His bones are lighter, longer and thinner.
He is less prominently muscled, and not nearly so powerful overall. He seldom scales more than 120 pounds.

The smallness of his head makes sense when one learns that it weighs considerably less than a leopard's head—less to carry. But with that small head go a small, weak jaw and the smallest and least menacing teeth of any of the larger carnivores. So equipped, cheetahs cannot afford to be aggressive animals. They are unable to protect their kills from leopards and are often driven off by hyenas as well.

The muzzle is short—again a weight saver—and the nostrils broad, an adaptation helpful in ensuring the quick delivery of oxygen to the lungs through nasal passages that are short and wide. This is an obvious advantage to a sprinter, whose peak oxygen demands may be very high. The skull is relatively light and high-domed, which permits the eye sockets to be set rather high in it. This arrangement is useful because it gives the animal an opportunity to see over the tops of the grasses while lying down, with a minimum exposure of himself.

The deep, narrow chest, with its long, light ribs, is capable of great expansion in breathing, again for maximum delivery of oxygen to the lungs. The lungs themselves are very large for the animal's weight. The rib cage also runs farther back than in most other mammals, thus providing even greater lung capacity—at the expense of the other internal organs. How these are tucked away in the cheetah is a kind of miracle, for he seems to have no belly at all. There is a dramatic narrowing of the body to a wasp waist that looks slender enough to be encircled by the fingers of two human hands. The legs are strangely long for a cat, and compared to a lion's or a leopard's they are as slender as matchsticks. No knots of sinew bulge from them, but the muscles are there nevertheless—long and flat and powerful, built for running.

Even the feet are specialized. The pads are small and tough like a dog's, with pronounced edges that aid in gripping the ground to avoid skids while following dodging prey. The toes are rather long, for that extra bit of leverage that a sprinter needs. The claws are only semi-retractile, like no other cat's. Their tips touch the ground, and in doing so they serve a double purpose. Not only do they act as extensions to the toes when running, but they also further improve traction, adding to the cheetah's ability to follow the twists and turns of a victim. They no longer have a primary use as weapons. Their constant contact with the ground blunts them; their role in gripping prey and in fighting is largely taken over by the dewclaws, which in cheetahs are large and very sharp.

The only thing that seems out of place in this marvelously honed running machine is the tail. This is an oddly luxurious and seemingly superfluous member, almost as long as the leopard's and appearing thicker in proportion to its length because it is bushier. Why does the cheetah need it? An answer is supplied by an American couple, Jule and Dan Mannix, who used to turn a pet cheetah loose in the western prairies to watch him chase jack rabbits. The jack rabbit is a super speedster too, capable of extraordinary acceleration, abrupt changes in direction and disconcerting leaps straight in the air. At first the Mannixes' cheetah was unable to catch jack rabbits; he was constantly dashing right under them as they leaped up over his head and took off in the opposite direction. But he quickly learned. And he used his tail for balance and as a rudder to help him turn quickly. It would go out stiffly to the side in the direction he wished to turn. If, in earning his living, a cheetah had only to run straight, the forces of natural selection would probably have shrunk his tail considerably by this time, and conceivably eliminated it. But he is such an efficient runner in all other respects that he can afford to keep his tail—in fact he needs it to help him control and direct the enormous speed that he has.

To match his splendid configuration, the cheetah is strikingly marked. His coat is not unlike a leopard's in appearance but is slightly coarser in texture. It comes in various shades of light golden brown, sometimes with a pale reddish cast, sometimes yellow, sometimes even a faint gray. It is darkest on the head and back, fading to white on the belly. The fur is heavily marked with black spots smaller then the leopard's rosettes, set more closely together and tending to be more uniform in size. The tail is also spotted, except at its end, which is encircled by one or two black bands. The very tip is white. The smallness of the head is matched by a pair of small rounded ears. The whiskers are short and sparse for a cat; a daylight hunter has little need for a large set. The cheetah's face is unforgettable. It has an expression all its own, centered on a pair of beautiful golden-brown eyes, darker than a lion's, wide-set, candid and serene. The upper brow is rather straight and does not have the slant that gives the cold green eye of the leopard its Satanic cast. The hairs around the eye are usually dark, and in some individuals black, making the eye seem larger than it is and the whole expression somewhat softer. Finally, running from the inner corner of each eye to the mouth is a bold black line. This warm golden face with its guileless eyes and those two striking black stripes is absolutely stunning. When it is combined with the way the animal moves and holds its head, it is overwhelmingly aristocratic and beautiful. Having such long legs, a cheetah, when he sits up, sits more vertically than other cats. His head is held high. He could be an aloof young desert prince,

proud with the pride of those who need no weapons, retinue or garments
to prove their worth, but who know it in themselves and show it in their car-
riage—their thoughts their own, their eyes on distant things.

Cheetahs speak their own language. Like other cats they are capable of
a variety of familiar snarling, yowling and spitting noises. But they often
communicate with one another with one sound that is uniquely theirs, a
high canarylike chirp. This has puzzled many people who are not familiar
with it. Theodore Roosevelt wrote: "When I first heard it I was sure that
it was uttered by some bird, and I looked about quite a time before finding that it was the call of a cheetah." Roosevelt also noted that the
cheetah twists his upper lip when chirping—as if whistling—but to my
knowledge this has not been confirmed by other writers.

Cheetah family life, what is known of it, appears to follow the normal pattern of most cats. When a female comes into heat she leaves her scent on
trees and bushes, and if there is a male in the neighborhood he quickly
turns up. There follows a brief honeymoon during which the two animals
are inseparable. They hunt together and are extremely affectionate. I have
no good information on whether the male stays with his spouse throughout
her pregnancy, which lasts about three months. One tame female cheetah
belonging to a professional game manager, Desmond Varaday, left him for
mating purposes, but came home again when her period of estrus was
over. However, her mate remained in the neighborhood, and may even
have still been there when her cubs were born, presumably to help feed
the family—Varaday is vague on the point. Furthermore, his pet, although
thoroughly domesticated, was also an accomplished hunter able to get
along on her own in the bush. This double life, with one foot in camp and
the other in the wild world, makes it dangerous to draw conclusions about
the habits of mated pairs from the behavior of this one. Of the cheetahs I
have seen, almost all of them were in pairs. I have no way of knowing whether they were honeymooners, post-honeymooners, or even members of the
same sex. But the frequency with which cheetahs are seen in pairs suggests that their liaisons are not the quick affairs of the leopard but may
last well beyond the honeymoon, perhaps right up through the birth and
rearing of the young.

A cheetah litter contains from two to five cubs. The species preserves its
reputation for oddity by producing young that look less like their parents
than is the case with any other cat. They are an entirely different color
than the adults, being covered with pale bluish-gray fur on their heads

and backs. This is rather long and shaggy, rising in a kind of ruff or mane above the shoulders and concealing the spots underneath. As a cub grows, this ruff becomes less prominent, but it persists even in adults, and is what helps give them their slightly humpbacked silhouette. A cub's flanks and legs are more conventionally cheetahlike. They are light brown and along with the rest of the body are covered with spots that become more visible as the animal grows bigger and loses its furry appearance.

But what marks a cheetah unmistakably from birth is the prominent black tear stripe running down from each eye. The effect of this stripe on the expression of an infant cheetah is surprising. In adults it merely adds distinction to what is already a distinctive and aristocratic face. But in some strange way the tear stripe makes the cheetah kitten look fierce. It stamps his face with a kind of permanent frown. Despite their unformed infantile features, baby cheetahs look comically determined and pugnacious. I once came across a mother with three very small cubs walking through the grass in the Amboseli Reserve. Whatever anxiety the mother may have felt, with her young out in the open, she betrayed nothing of it. She strolled along with that imperturbable air of serenity that is so much the mark of the cheetah, but her tiny cubs plodded after her, the very embodiment of infant ferocity. In a minute or two the mother had steered them into a thick clump of bushes. I have a photograph of the mother sitting there, gazing calmly off into space, with one of her babies scowling out of the thicket. The contrast in the two expressions is astonishing.

Cheetah cubs are relatively short-legged and chunky at first. Their claws are sharp and, like all cats, they are excellent climbers. Stevenson-Hamilton had two that could swarm up the wire mesh of a cage they were kept in, and could even cling upside down to the top. However, walking around soon blunts their claws, and by the time they are adults they have lost most of their ability to climb. But this does not keep them from trying. They like elevations and are often found lying on top of anthills from which they can survey the surrounding countryside. If there is a handy tree with a sloping trunk, they will bound up it. But they are not really at home in trees. When hard-pressed by dogs they may attempt to climb them, but they may be unable to do so. Even the most ponderous lions are better climbers than cheetahs are.

Young cheetahs grow rapidly and at 10 months are leggy adolescents, nearly as big as their mother but with none of her dignity. Already they can run like the wind, but they must be taught how to hunt and kill. Like adolescents everywhere, their attention span is short, and much of their

energy is spent chasing and skylarking with one another. But by the time
they are two years old they are indistinguishable from their mother both
in size and behavior. Since groups of five and six cheetahs are sometimes
seen traveling and hunting together, this has given rise to the belief that
they form prides like lions. This is not so; the groups are families—still together, but about to break up and go their separate ways.

Whether a cheetah hunts alone or as a member of a family band, his technique is much the same. If the terrain offers concealment, an effort will be
made to creep close before the final rush is made. Or the hunter will walk
or trot, seemingly aimlessly, in an effort to get within striking range. At
first his gait may appear innocuously slow. But once he has picked out a particular individual in the herd, he will increase his pace imperceptibly, and
when he thinks he is close enough he will suddenly explode with everything
he has. Two or three jumps and he is flying at top speed. If his quarry is
not supremely alert, and does not burst into flight the instant the cheetah
takes off, then the pursuer will make up that last critical hundred yards or
so, and the antelope is doomed. But antelopes who live beyond babyhood
are supremely alert and many of a cheetah's spectacular rushes end in failure. Finding that he is not closing fast enough, he will break off his
pursuit as suddenly as he started it and will pace about for a minute or
two "in a towering rage" as one writer put it. Whether this is really anger
or simply the kind of restless walking about that an athlete engages in
while recovering his breath after a peak effort in a race is not certain. Cheetahs, as will be noted, are not quite as serene-tempered as they appear to
be on the surface, and it may be that they are simply cooling out. And,
short though their staying-power is, their recovery time is also short. More
than one observer has watched a cheetah hurl himself into a blistering
chase within minutes of an equally blistering one that earned him nothing.

If he catches something, once again the cheetah is an individualist; his eating habits differ from those of the lion and leopard in several respects. He
is a sloppy feeder, and a trained observer can recognize a cheetah kill from
its mangled condition and from the fact that the entrails have been rough-
ly torn out, and not removed and buried, as is the usual habit of the lion
or leopard. A second peculiarity: cheetahs seldom return to their kills.
They do not like rotten meat, and thus can get only one meal from a prey animal. This puts a strain on them as hunters—as it does on the game—
because they have to kill more often than the less discriminating lion or
leopard. Finally, cheetahs eat where they kill. Not only are they less pow-

(continued on page 149)

Right front pawprint of cheetah

THE CHEETAH

His eyes a deep golden brown, in contrast to the pitiless yellow or green of the lion and leopard, the cheetah has a much gentler expression than either of his larger cousins. This is accentuated by the beautiful lyre-shaped pattern caused by the black lines that run from the inner corner of each eye down to the mouth. His head is also much smaller in proportion to his body. His jaw is small and relatively weak, his teeth correspondingly small, his neck slender. His whiskers are short and droopy; being an animal who hunts by sight and in daylight, he probably does not need whiskers at all, and those that he has are mere leftovers from a time when his ancestors followed a life that was more conventionally catlike. But the cheetah today has departed from the traditionally catlike way of making a living. He is a courser, not a stalker, and his whole body has become lightened, attenuated, specialized for tremendous bursts of speed. For an understanding of what is meant structurally by the concept "cheetah," one need only glance at a picture of a cheetah running at top speed (*next page*). Instantly all his specialized parts, seemingly rather awkward in repose, fuse to make him one of the most dazzling, graceful animals in existence.

As a runner, the cheetah is capable of explosive acceleration and has been clocked at speeds of 60 miles an hour for a quarter of a mile. He covers the ground in enormous bounds of 25 feet, his hind legs giving him tremendous thrust, which is increased by a very flexible backbone that uncoils to hurl his body forward as he stretches out in mid-leap. He touches the ground with only one paw at a time, landing first on one forepaw, then striding forward to the other while he is gathering his hindquarters under him. Then, at maximum compression of his body, one hind foot will touch the ground; the body will start to uncoil and shoot forward as the other hind foot touches down. In the remarkable picture on the previous page of a wild cheetah running at full tilt, the hind quarters have been tucked forward with the body in the "coiled" position. The left hind foot is stretched forward as far as the chest and about to hit the ground. The picture below shows a cheetah with only his right forefoot in contact with the ground and his hind feet being gathered under him for the next jump. This photograph is of a tame animal released to chase a herd of impala. It is remarkable in that of the eight animals in the left of the picture, all are in full leap, without a single hoof touching the ground. Impala are very fast themselves; the cheetah failed to get a good jump on them and they all got away.

When cheetahs hunt in pairs they can cut down the advantage that a small zigzagging animal might have. In the picture above, they have closed in on a hare. The cheetah at left has cuffed it into the air, and his partner, in an extraordinary change of direction that would do credit to a hockey player, is swerving to grab it. Opposite, a mother with grown cubs feeds on a kill. Then, like all cats everywhere, they end off their meal with a drink.

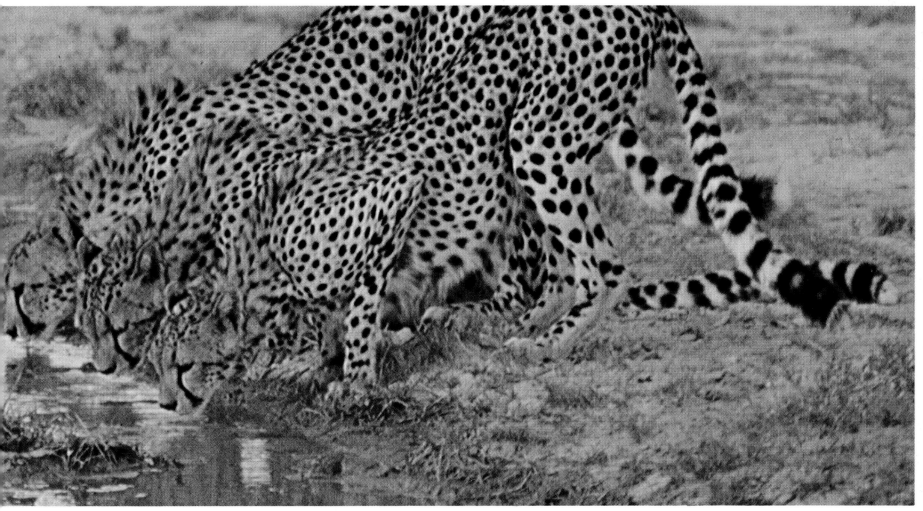

Because his legs are so long in proportion
to the rest of his body, a cheetah, when
he sits up, is in a much more nearly vertical
position than would be the case with other
cats. The benign expression of the two
adults shown here is in curious contrast
to that of the small cub below. The facial
stripes, the intent expression of his eye
and the set of his jaw give him a
pugnacious look that is utterly lacking in
his parents. He also is born with a quantity
of long, shaggy, grayish hair around his
head and back. This gradually dwindles
to a small mane in adults. Groups of
cheetahs that yawn and stretch and nuzzle
like lion prides (*next page*) are not prides
at all, but grown families that have not
yet split up.

It takes about two years for a family of
young cheetahs to grow up, learn what
they must learn about hunting and depart
to find mates of their own. During the
last six months or more before the family
breakup the young ones are as large as
their parents, which is what has given rise
to the belief that cheetahs actually form
prides. One way of spotting an adolescent
cheetah is that the ruff on the back of his
neck is more prominent (*left, below*) than
that of an adult.

erful than their larger relatives, so that dragging a heavy carcass more than a few yards presents a serious physical challenge to them, but they also have to eat fairly promptly. News travels fast on the savanna, and alert eyes and noses may bring a big rival on the scene before the cheetah has fairly gotten into his dinner. So he dines on the spot.

The extent to which animals watch each other, and the things they are able to learn from watching, is greater than is generally realized. The gathering of vultures over a nearby cheetah kill may mean the difference between one more meal and starvation to an old but observant lion, his wits sharpened by necessity as he approaches the end of his days. More subtle is how one animal will read the intent of another in ways that humans do not comprehend. With some friends I once saw two cheetahs strolling in the Mara Reserve. Strolling discreetly behind them was a jackal.

"That jackal trailing along means that they're hunting," said Bob Lowis.

"How does he know that?" I asked.

"I don't know, but he does."

We decided to trail along too, even more discreetly. For a couple of miles we crept along in the Land Rover while the cheetahs walked steadily but with no apparent purpose across country. They ignored various clusters of antelope scattered about the landscape. They also ignored the jackal, but he was obviously getting some kind of message because he stubbornly tagged along. Then we paused for a moment to look at a kori bustard, an enormous bird of the savanna, who was also strolling. When we looked around for the cheetahs they had disappeared. Fifteen minutes later we found them again. Acting as a lion might, we investigated a rapid gathering of vultures on the nearby horizon, and there the cheetahs were, just starting to feed on a freshly killed wildebeest calf. The jackal was sitting to one side, patiently waiting. By only a moment's inattention we had missed the rare sight of a cheetah kill. To make matters worse, a lion did come up and the cheetahs ran off. But the jackal was bolder. He got in a few mouthfuls before the lion arrived, and then sat down patiently to wait for his second course. To man, one cheetah going somewhere looks like another cheetah going somewhere. But this apparently is not the case with jackals, for they do not always follow cheetahs—they do it only when there is something in it for them.

Cheetahs almost identical with the modern ones have existed for at least three million years. A few million years before that, as the chart on page

27 shows, nothing like a cheetah had yet put in an appearance. Sometime between these two dates certain of the more generalized early cats found that they were swift enough to run down some of the less specialized early herbivores. With other cats growing in size and strength to specialize in the stalk and sudden spring, there was a niche open for a running cat. The fastest and rangiest of these cats were the most successful, and eventually the modern cheetah emerged. During this same period, of course, the herbivores were not exactly standing still. They became swifter too—both hunter and hunted being stimulated by each other to new peaks of evolutionary efficiency.

Having reached something resembling his present form, the cheetah occupied a range that extended throughout the warmer grassland areas of the Africa-Asia land mass. There were dramatic climatic changes during this period, with rivers running and game herds flourishing in what is now the Sahara. But the herds moved with the changes, and the cheetah with them. In historic times cheetahs have been found in suitable open country throughout Africa and eastward through Arabia, Persia, Turkestan and India. Predictably, the "splitters" and "lumpers" among scientists have had their innings in trying to sort out the various types. In this case it appears that the latter have won; today all living cheetahs are usually "lumped" in a single species. For a while it was believed that a second and much rarer species with stripes on the back existed in Rhodesia, but taxonomists have now come to the conclusion that these are simply oddly marked members of the main group.

The gentle, aristocratic bearing that is so apparent in the cheetah is not misleading. Although there are great personality variations from individual to individual, as there are among all higher animals, cheetahs as a whole are amiable and mild mannered. They are easily tamed, and have been used as pets and as coursing animals by humans for nearly four thousand years. Pictures of cheetahs wearing collars and leashes have been found in Egyptian tombs that go back to 1500 B.C., and their earliest domestication probably antedates those pictures by a couple of centuries at least. Frederick E. Zeuner, who has made a specialty of determining how and when animals were first domesticated, believes that Egypt is where tame cheetahs were first known and that their use as hunting animals spread from there to Assyria, India and central Asia.

They have been the playthings of royalty through the centuries. King Hashing of Persia kept cheetahs in 865 B.C. The Romans, with their passion for importing exotic animals, knew them well. After the fall of Rome they cropped up in North Africa in the retinues of Vandal kings. They also made their way east as far as China where Kublai Khan, according to Marco Polo, "hath numbers . . . trained to the chase." But nobody outdid Akbar the Great, the Mogul ruler of India in the 16th Century. The often-printed claim that his hunting establishment contained a thousand cheetahs is surely exaggeration. But the sheer size of the exaggeration makes it fairly certain that he had a great many of them. The most celebrated of Akbar's cheetahs was named Semend-Manik, and it was carried to the hunting field in its own palanquin, preceded by a servant who proclaimed its importance by banging on a kettledrum.

Cheetahs were also very popular in the French and Italian courts during the Renaissance, where they satisfied much the same desire of the nobility for an elegant and exclusive sport that was satisfied by hawking. Both required money, servants, leisure time and a willingness to lavish all three on the careful training of the cheetah or falcon and on the gradual building up of a complex code of standards and performance. The use of sporting dogs today for field trials is—psychologically—identical with the earlier use of cheetahs and hawks. The only difference is that 500 years ago the chase was the exclusive province of the nobility; a commoner caught killing game was liable to be killed himself. Today anybody who wants to train a pointer or a retriever and shoot over it can do so. But now that the exclusivity is gone—when anybody can get into the club—the desirability of the club begins to fade. It is unlikely that field trials will last for 3,500 years, as cheetah coursing did; the status simply isn't there. To own a cheetah, a man really had to be somebody, and his cheetah showed it, just as a 12-meter yacht or a Rolls Royce does for some modern Americans (or would if only a tiny fraction of the population was allowed by law to own Rolls Royces). Louis XI of France, by his own edict, was the only man in his entire realm permitted to own and use hunting cheetahs—*there* was a status symbol that no Rolls Royce could match, and it probably cost more in the money of the day than a Rolls Royce does now. When Louis wanted a cheetah he had to send to Ethiopia or some equally exotic place for it—and if he wanted another, he had to send for that one too, because cheetahs rarely breed in captivity.

The use of cheetahs in the hunting field has changed little. In ancient Egypt men would ride out, with their cheetahs trotting alongside attached by long leashes. When game was sighted the leashes would be slipped, and off the animals would go. Later practice favored transporting them in small carts. They wore hoods over their heads, just like falcons, and these would be removed in the presence of game. Unhooded, a cheetah would sight its quarry, leap from the cart with a tremendous bound and quickly run it down. It was trained not to mangle its kill, and would be rewarded with a cup of fresh blood from the victim's throat. Sometimes a cheetah could be trained to sit behind his master on an extension of the saddle. The Emperor Frederick II of Sicily, who introduced the sport to Europe, had several that could do this.

Coursing with cheetahs continued into modern times in Persia, Arabia and India, the last practitioners of all being sports-minded maharajahs. But by the end of the 19th Century the species had become so rare in Asia that the agents of the maharajahs were turning up in Africa in increasing numbers, looking for specimens to train. Cheetahs are not particularly difficult to catch, but in the initial fury of being caught they often damage themselves unless they are handled with great skill. In the past this led to a high mortality rate and contributed to the rapid disappearance of the species, since it often took a number of wild cheetahs to deliver one live healthy captive.

There are two principal ways of capturing wild specimens. They can be run down by men on horseback (which is surprising, considering their speed, and will be explained shortly). The usual method is to snare them. Like many cats, they have favorite scratching trees. When such a tree has been located, it is surrounded by snares that will catch one or more of the animal's feet when he comes to scratch. Some people insist that cheetahs should be taken young if they are to be trained in coursing. But most authorities believe that they need to be taught how to kill by their mother while still in the wild state, and that the best coursers are those captured and trained as adults. The latter belief would seem to be the more logical, considering the species' tractability.

Today, if not extinct in Asia, the cheetah is so nearly so that for all practical purposes it can be considered a doomed species on that continent. It is only poetic justice that the maharajahs are nearly extinct also.

In Africa the cheetah hangs on, but his hold is a precarious one. The times are against him and so is his own nature. Despite his being the gentlest and most tractable of the big cats, he is also the most detached. He likes attention, and solicits it, but underneath he remains cool. Michaela Denis, who has raised both cheetah and leopard, came to the surprising discovery that her leopard was noticeably the warmer and more affectionate of the two. Not necessarily the easier, but the more responsive. Further, the cheetah's disposition, for all its apparent amiability, is often very tight-ly strung. He is easily upset, and sometimes gives vent to the kind of seemingly senseless hair-trigger violence against other cheetahs than can flare up between a couple of insanely proud young aristocrats like Shakespeare's Mercutio and Tybalt.

It is tempting to carry this analogy a little further, in that the cheetah has both an unpredictable temper and an aristocratic hauteur. But his seems to be the hauteur of an aristocracy that has been bred too fine, that is approaching the point of fragility, the inability to cope—when the blood has become too thin and too blue. Lions and leopards will fight for life until they are quite literally dead; cheetahs may simply give up, and it is this characteristic that makes hunting them on horseback possible. Here is a seeming illogicality. A cheetah can run twice as fast as a horse, and if it had a mind to, could simply disappear over the horizon while the horse was getting up speed. But too often for its own good it does not, as has been attested by numerous detailed reports. A couple of these come from Frederick Courteney Selous, one of the reliable early naturalists writing from Africa at the turn of the century. Once Selous and a friend came upon three cheetahs, a male and two females, in open country. Being well mounted the men decided to try and run them down. Somewhat to their surprise, instead of falling behind, they gained a little on the cheetahs, which seemed content merely to keep ahead of the hunters. Suddenly both females stopped, so suddenly that Selous and his companion, intent on the larger male, rushed right by. A few moments later the male abruptly stopped too and lay flat on the ground. Selous galloped some distance past before he was able to rein in his horse, but the cheetah never moved. Nor did it when Selous dismounted, walked up to it and shot it. On another occasion, his companion's horse jumped right over a cheetah that suddenly stopped running and crouched on the ground. Again it never moved, but waited for the hunter to return and shoot it.

What was most puzzling to Selous was that he and his friends, mounted as they were, never succeeded in catching any of the antelope that cheetahs were able to catch.

Why does a cheetah suddenly give in? Why does he wait resignedly for a man to dismount, walk up to him and shoot him when he could certainly take advantage of the opportunity to run off in another direction? Is it hauteur carried to the nth degree, a thin-blooded relinquishing of the will to live? Unfortunately for the analogy, and for all similar attempts to interpret animal behavior in terms of human values, it is not. If the behavior seems quixotic or abnormal, it must be remembered that the situation, from the cheetah's point of view, was also abnormal. A proper explanation must be sought in the cheetah's ability to deal with new challenges. Being the most specialized of all the cats, he is also the most limited in the kinds of response he can make to a given situation. He cannot fight very well, having weak jaws and teeth. He is a poor tree climber. He cannot run for very long. Most important, he cannot think any but certain thoughts. He evolved into what he is in an environment that for many thousands of years contained no enemy that would even consider trying to catch him by running after him. Therefore, it is asking too much of the intelligence of a cheetah, in his first experience with mounted human hunters, to understand that it is dangerous for him to run just fast enough to keep ahead of them. How is he to know that his salvation lies in a desperate burst of initial speed in an effort to get clear away? He cannot know it, so he just bounds off. But his internal chemistry is not built for sustained bounding. A moment comes when he can bound no more. Having run out of wind, he is defenseless. It is as unfair to criticize him for this as it is to criticize an old elephant for starving to death because its teeth have become so worn down that it can no longer chew.

In the introduction to this book it was pointed out that cats, as a group, are relatively unspecialized, and that that is one of the reasons why they have been as successful as they are. They are intelligent, and they are adaptable. The cheetah may be the least intelligent of the true cats, and is certainly the least adaptable. He is neither an amiable opportunist like the lion nor a saturnine one like the leopard; in a rapidly changing world his outlook is the bleakest.

In Africa his numbers are now sadly reduced. He is completely gone from North Africa, probably absent from Ethiopia, and is almost exterminated in South Africa, where he has been heavily hunted on the questionable charge of being a hazard to domestic stock. He hangs on in rather small numbers in East Africa, mostly in the game parks. But even there he may have his troubles. Being a diurnal hunter, he is up and about when the sightseers and photographers are also on the move. And in their zeal to get close to a cheetah they may well interfere with his hunting. So far, this is not a serious problem, for the human traffic in the game parks is not all that heavy. But it will grow; indeed the present governments of Kenya and Tanzania are committed to a massive growth of tourism as a mainstay of their economies. And if the human tide, however respectful it may be, should ever approach the level now experienced in the Nairobi Park, where a pride of lions is "passed on" by word of mouth from one party of observers to another and remains ringed by eager watchers throughout the daylight hours—then the hunting cheetah will find it nearly impossible to make a living.

A cheetah does the bulk of his hunting in the hours after sunrise and just before sunset, and his survival chances would be immeasurably improved if a way were found to keep certain areas free of visitors during those critical times of the day. But one thing is sure. Unless expanses of open savanna are preserved and stocked with the game that the cheetah can utilize—and where he can put to proper use the one talent he has: running like the wind—he will quickly become extinct.

THE SMALLER CATS

In addition to the big three—lion, leopard and cheetah—Africa contains seven other cats. Or, more properly, eight, for the domestic tabby is now found throughout the continent, and, although descended recently from an existing wild species and still resembling it very closely, it is now generally regarded as a true species on its own.

These eight smaller cats all belong to a single genus, *Felis*. What distinguishes them from their bigger brothers in the genus *Leo?* Are there any consistent anatomical differences that justify this grouping? The answer, of course, is yes—for it is such differences that form the basis for the classification of all living things. In the case of the cats, the important differences are two. And they have nothing to do with size, color or habits, for in these respects the little cats are as different from one another as the big ones. The first difference, in fact, is not visible at all from the outside; it has to do with the windpipe. In the genus *Felis* this is connected directly to the skull by some small bones called the hyoid bones. In *Leo* there is a ligament between the hyoid bones and the skull. This difference may seem inconsequential, but it is not. The ligament provides a certain amount of elasticity to the windpipe, which is what makes it possible for the big cats to roar. And it is this difference that suggested to Charles Guggisberg, the Kenya lion expert, that they should be called "roaring cats" and the little ones "purring cats." These labels are handy and vivid, but not 100 per cent applicable. Although the elastic connection to the hyoid bones does provide a kind of sounding box that makes roaring possible, the lion is the only large cat that takes complete advantage of his capability. The others are notably quiet, and for the most part content themselves with low "conversation" in addition to a variety of coughing grunts and snarls that they emit when angry.

For the smaller cats, however, the label is most apt. They all purr. They also yowl, moan, hiss and spit, but there is not a roar in the lot.

The second difference between *Felis* and *Leo* is in the eye. All cats have round pupils, but the contracting apparatus is not the same. Among the big cats it resembles that of humans—in bright light the pupil gets smaller, but it remains round. Among the small cats it narrows to a slit.

So much for the structural differences. There are others less precisely measurable, of which temperament is perhaps the one most worth commenting on. The small African cats are noticeably more vicious than the big ones and —with the single exception of the house cat—they are far more difficult to tame. This is surprising. One would think that the great cats, with their enormous strength, their implacable way of hunting, their ferocity toward one another when angry and their occasional deadliness as man-eaters, would be the untamable ones. On the contrary, their very size apparently makes it less necessary for them to be constantly on the alert to defend themselves, and this gives them a reserve of assurance, or at least a greater feeling of relaxation than seems present in the smaller ones. It has even been suggested by Franz A. Roedelberger and Vera I. Groschoff that the small cats, since they are capable of catching only small prey, have to hunt more regularly—perhaps as often as 10 or 20 times a day—and as a result are kept in a more constant state of nervous tension.

Whatever the reason, big cats are tamable; small ones (with a few individual exceptions) are not. The ease with which cheetahs can be tamed has already been described, and to a reading and movie-going public that has been exposed to Joy Adamson's famous Elsa, it should come as no surprise that lions make good pets. In fact, zoos around the world are populated with lions that have been reared in private homes as cubs and only parted with because of the tremendous problem of trying to fit 400-pound pets into human communities—to say nothing of the fact that most communities have laws against it.

What may be surprising is that even a leopard can make a good pet. Helen Martini, wife of the lion keeper at New York's Bronx Zoo, succeeded in raising one. Furthermore, this animal was a black one, supposed to be the worst of all. Nevertheless, Mrs. Martini took the cub in and had tremendous success with it. She returned it to the zoo after it was grown —which was just as well, since the Martinis lived in a small apartment surrounded by uneasy neighbors—but it retained its affection for her. She would visit it whenever she went to the zoo and would stroke it through the bars, to the great astonishment of visitors, and to the great joy of the leopard. At night, when nobody was around to see her, she would often take it for walks on a leash, and once, overdue for supper, she was found by her anxious husband sitting in a tree with it. The leopard had indicated that he wanted her to, so she did.

Another celebrated leopard pet was raised by Armand Denis' wife, Michaela. It, too, was a complex and fascinating creature and from the beginning showed a great capacity for affection and a need of attention. This animal, Tshui, grew to full size in the Denises' care and developed only one questionable social habit; it liked to stalk visitors in the Denises' garden and leap on them. This was all done in play and with the claws sheathed, but it was highly unnerving to the Denises' guests. This cat, too, wound up in a zoo, for there always lurks the possibility that a human being engaged in play with a big cat may not understand the rules of the game as the cat understands them and may unwittingly do something to trigger a violent response. Something of this sort happened in the case cited in John Dominis' foreword to this book. But for the good name of all leopards, it should be pointed out that the animal that so savagely clawed that teenage girl was not really tame in the sense that it spent the greater part of its time freely with people, trusted them and was trusted by them in return. It was never a true pet.

With real intimacy comes real trust, and it is over this line that the small African cats seem reluctant to step. Whether caught as adults or raised as kittens, they remain sullen and suspicious. They do not like to be handled, and the best that comes out of a relationship between a human and one of these unreconstructed little African spitfires is an armed truce. Individual cases to the contrary exist but, by and large, the smaller African cats are extremely touchy customers.

One last generalization can be made about these cats: remarkably little is known about them. This is not surprising, considering their nocturnal habits and their general dislike and distrust of man. But that is not the whole story. They are relatively easy to trap, many of them do well in captivity, and kittens often fall into the hands of hunters or villagers who have killed their parents. Still, no detailed study has ever been made of any one of them in the wild. Armand Denis has made the telling observation that our knowledge of the cats of Africa "is directly proportional to their size." This is very curious. It must be due in some measure to the human fascination with bigness, which is a pity, because the small cats are as varied, and probably as interesting, as the large ones. I say "probably" because no one really knows all that much about them. They go their own intense little ways in considerable obscurity; their ranges are not clearly defined; the secrets of their private lives remain unprobed; even their numbers are not accurately known. Some may be far more numerous than is suspected; others may be on the brink of extinction.

Applying Denis' law of diminishing knowledge with diminishing size, one could assume that the middle-sized cats are middling known, and that turns out to be true. There are two of these welterweights, the serval and caracal. They represent a considerable drop in size from the leopard and cheetah, being in the 30-40 pound class. The others are smaller still. They are mostly the size of house cats and seldom weigh more than 10 pounds.

One afternoon, out late, when the thick, high grass along one of the Serengeti watercourses was turned to gold by the low sun, I saw at some distance a spotted animal, as yellow as the grass, walking sedately along. Thoughts of leopard, then of cheetah, flashed through my mind but were as quickly banished. This animal was too small to be either, and somehow looked "wrong" even at that distance. I got my binoculars on it and quickly found that it was indeed wrong in several respects. It looked like no cat I had ever seen before. It had something of the long-legged, spare build of a cheetah, and had a cheetah's spots, but otherwise it bore no resemblance to a cheetah at all. There were some uncheetahlike stripes on its back, and its tail was so short that it failed to reach the ground even when hanging straight down. But most unusual was its head. Its muzzle was sharply pointed for a cat. Its ears were preposterously large and batlike—so wide at the base that they almost met in the middle of the head.

It was a serval. I saw it for only a minute or two, but even during that short glimpse it managed to convey a strong sense of its own individuality and character—yet another cat, with another shape and another way of life. A week later I saw a second one, and was again struck by its individuality. Once seen and fixed in the mind's eye, a serval can be nothing else. This is a graceful and dainty animal whose long legs and large ears give some hints—which I later confirmed by reading—as to how the serval makes his living.

The first thing I learned was that he belonged where I had seen him: in thick grass and bushy cover near streams. This gives him the privacy and concealment he desires for lying up during the day. It also provides the kind of environment preferred by the creatures he preys on: cane rats, hares, lizards, guinea fowl and other game birds, and the young of the smallest antelopes. These are usually found near water, particularly where there is a rather abrupt change from thick to more open vegetation. In a New England woodland the greatest variety and concentration of small animals and birds is found neither in the forest nor in the open meadow, but in the mixed growth that forms the dividing line between the two zones. Somewhat the same situation prevails along the African watercourses, where there is a transition from the thick tangle of mixed cover that lines the stream itself to the open grassy stretches of the savanna. It is under the bushes that the big flocks of guinea fowl and the francolin live, and from which they emerge to feed, going back again at night to roost in the low branches of the trees. The tall grasses are alive with rats and hares.

Given this environment, what would be the best feline design for exploiting it? With all that small game moving about in the thick cover, the predator should certainly be one that depended on speed and dexterity rather than on strength. It should be tall enough to see over the tops of the grasses. And to trace the movements of rats and mice creeping unseen down at grassroot level, it would need excellent hearing. This is the serval design—long-legged, big-eared, not powerful, but very, very quick.

So equipped, the serval is capable of one specialized kind of hunting that must be marvelous to see. Suspecting the presence of small game in a patch of grass, or in the hope of scaring some up, he will leap over the tops of the grass in a series of beautiful arabesques, turning and twisting, his paws tucked in, his body arched, his ears pricked forward. Back and forth he will go. And with that menacing shadow bounding overhead, the urge to bolt must be very great in any small rodent that happens to be cowering in the area. Rigid, motionless, with all its small muscles gathered, it will lie low, waiting, hoping with the hope that only a defenseless animal can know, that it will pass unnoticed. But sooner or later one of those floating random leaps will come too close for the steadiest of rodent nerves. There will be a sudden scuttle. That is all the serval needs. His dexterity and speed are so great that a small prey animal, once it has been detected, scarcely ever escapes.

That all servals hunt in this fashion remains to be demonstrated. The pictures shown on pages 166-171 are the only ones of their kind ever taken and represent evidence that has not yet found acceptance among mammalogists. This is not so much because anyone doubts that this is a usual hunting technique among servals as it is simply a failure to spend enough time observing them to make absolutely sure.

In his leaping the serval is a kind of courser who depends not so much on stalking and ambush as he does on stirring up his prey and then catching it. Reflecting this, he is the cat that most closely resembles the cheetah in configuration, although his specialization is not nearly so extreme. And like the cheetah, his staying power is short. If he should start a dik-dik or a large hare that gets a good jump on him, he will quickly give up the chase if it goes more than a few hundred yards.

Servals are excellent climbers. They take their share of roosting birds in trees and are also reputed able to catch hyraxes, those strange woodchuck-sized and woodchuck-shaped arboreal animals of tropical Africa that look like rodents but whose nearest living relatives are—puzzlingly—elephants.

The serval follows the familiar cat pattern whereby the male and female separate after breeding. The female usually bears three kittens, which she rears in a den in the rocks or often in the abandoned hole of an aardvark or porcupine. When the young are old enough to fend for themselves the family breaks up. Servals are shy animals but are attracted to farms and native villages by the ease with which they can find and kill poultry there. All-black individuals are occasionally found. As with leopards, this melanistic strain runs strongest in cool or mountainous areas. Again, as with leopards, its selective advantage is not known.

The second of the middle-sized African cats is the caracal, or African lynx. I earlier spoke out for the cheetah as the most beautiful and stirring of all the cats. But I have never seen a caracal, and from what others say about him, and from what John Dominis' pictures show, he is certainly a stunning animal—perhaps the most stunning of all. He is one of the few unpatterned cats. He is a bright reddish brown, becoming white on the belly, which sometimes shows a few brownish spots; otherwise his coat is unmarked. His tail is short, even shorter than the serval's.

The caracal's head is dramatically beautiful, wider than the serval's and more conventionally catlike in its proportions. The eyes are large and baleful, with the color and uncompromising expression of a leopard's, and with a prominent black spot over each. The white of the underparts extends upward to the chin and around the lips, which are edged with black. The ears are large and pointed, each with a tuft of long hairs at the tip. These tufts sometimes stand up straight, making the ears seem even larger than they are; sometimes they hang down like graceful little tassels.

For his size the caracal is an extremely powerful and savage animal. As the leopard is to the cheetah, so is the caracal to the serval—no bigger, but heavier and much tougher. He is widely distributed in Africa, preferring semi-arid thorn bush country. He feeds on much the same prey as the serval, but being stronger and more leopardlike in his habits he winds up

(continued on page 177)

Right front pawprint of serval   Right front pawprint of caracal

THE SERVAL and CARACAL

The serval and the caracal, together with five still-smaller cats, represent the genus *Felis* in Africa. They all have the hyoid bone structure in the throat that makes purring possible, and they also have in common the distinguishing characteristic of possessing eye pupils that narrow to a slit—just like those of the house cat, which descended originally from one of the small wild African cats. The largest members of this genus are the serval *(right)* and the caracal *(pages 172-176)*. Bat-eared, daintily long-legged, with a thick short tail and a sharply pointed muzzle that is more like a fox's than a cat's, the serval is a markedly graceful animal. Largely nocturnal, it is sometimes seen at dawn or dusk, particularly in cool, cloudy weather. Under ordinary circumstances, one might spend many years trying to photograph a wild serval, so John Dominis decided to make these pictures of a partly tamed captive one that had all of the characteristics of a wild animal but was sufficiently accustomed to human beings so that it would behave naturally and unselfconsciously in front of his camera.

Although he catches a variety of small game by the traditional cat method of stalk and pounce and even climbs trees after roosting birds, small monkeys and hyraxes, the serval has developed one method of hunting that is all his own. In an area of thick matted grass, which is ideal cover for hares and rodents, he will execute a series of graceful leaps. Back and forth he will jump, looking and listening, with his big bat ears pricked forward, for any frightened stir of movement in the grass. Once something moves, his reflexes are fast enough to enable him to pounce on it. These pictures are believed to be the first ever taken showing the serval engaged in his peculiar hunting technique.

How the serval's jumping technique pays off is shown in this sequence. In the first picture at left, he is simply jumping about idly—hoping. But he has already come dangerously close to a hare that is alert, frightened and just about to bolt. A fraction of a second later the hare moves, and the serval, still in mid-air, instantly spots it. In short order he will pounce on it and kill it with a bite in the neck. Then he will lie down, as shown below, to hug it possessively for a moment before eating it. If the hare had been better hidden, or if the serval had jumped the other way, the story would have been different; the thickets of Africa are full of small animals that servals never see at all.

Another serval technique depends on acute hearing, patience and lightning-fast reflexes. In the picture at far left, the serval has detected the presence of a mole rat in its burrow. He places himself above the burrow entrance, one paw raised, ready to strike. Here he waits like a statue until the rat decides that things are safe enough above ground to poke its nose out. With one rapierlike scoop, the serval sends the rat spinning into the air *(top picture, this page),* rears up to follow its flight, and is ready to pounce on the rat as it comes down. This is the kind of small game that the serval, a lightly constructed and not particularly strong animal, is best suited to prey on. Inasmuch as a rat or mouse makes a small meal, the serval will have to hunt rather steadily, particularly if it is a female raising kittens. This hunting pressure keeps the serval keyed up, and some scientists believe that is why it is so much more difficult to tame than the supposedly more ferocious, but actually more relaxed, big cats.

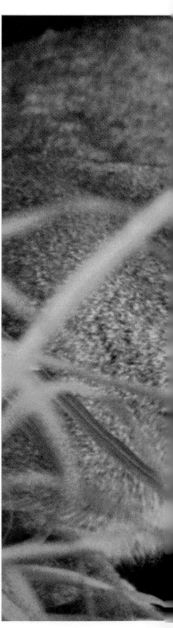

Strikingly colored, and with dramatic tufts on the tips of his ears, the caracal is one of the most distinctive cats in the world. Related to the lynxes of the Northern Hemisphere, he is about the size of a serval but is considerably stronger, and noticeably more intractable. The female photographed here never did get used to John Dominis, and he had great difficulty in getting any pictures of her at all. The problem was intensified by the fact that she had a kitten (*below*) that she felt extremely nervous about. Dominis finally put cat and kitten in a large enclosure full of natural cover and waited patiently to get his pictures when the cat showed herself.

One thing that lured the caracal out of the thick bushes was the presence of wild doves in her enclosure. She would hear them moving about, and would quietly stalk them with infinite care. When within a few feet of them, she would suddenly spring into their midst. The doves would take off in all directions, but the cat was so quick that she could usually knock down one or two of them before they flew out of reach. A quick stab with claws extended (*left*), a clutch and a bite (*below*) and the dove would be hers. Dominis burned off dozens of rolls of film getting these pictures and considers this the most difficult part of his entire assignment. What the caracal thought of him is shown on the next page.

with fewer rats and mice and more antelopes. A good climber, he kills many roosting birds, even eagles, and is so quick with his paws that he can snatch in the air birds that he has flushed from the ground.

The caracal is the only one of the smaller cats reputed to attack humans when disturbed at a kill. In captivity he is notoriously intractable, and is probably the least likely of all the African cats, large or small, to make a satisfactory pet. This has not kept people from trying, and it is only proper to mention that "tame" caracals have been reported—although their tameness is of a highly qualified character. Peter Molloy, when he was a game warden in the Southern Sudan, had a caracal that as a youngster would romp with his dog. It also became very attached to Molloy and even as an adult enjoyed being fondled, but, significantly, it was kept in a cage. Armand Denis, who seems to have owned every kind of cat at one time or another, has had personal experiences with both serval and caracal. Of the serval he writes: "They are playful, fascinating pets as long as you realize that they are unlikely ever to lose their basic wildness. Their public relations with other pets [are] deplorable." The best he could say of his caracal, which had "fits of wildness," was that it could be calmed down with a saucer of milk. Stevenson-Hamilton once met a lady in Portuguese East Africa who had a caracal that would sit in her lap—but in nobody else's. Several that he had himself were all untamable.

This is the kind of grudging, qualified endorsement that one keeps running into in the accounts of those who have kept caracals. It is surprising, therefore, to hear from Stanley H. Prater, reporting from India, that the caracal there is as easily tamed as the cheetah and was "once popular in Persia" as a hunting animal. I cannot comment on this except to note that the way in which these hunting caracals were supposedly employed is entirely in keeping with their physical capabilities. They were used to catch birds. Turned loose on a flock of feeding pigeons, a champion performer could supposedly bat down nine or 10 before they could get away.

The caracal photographed in this book was a captive female. She turned out to be a representative member of her species. Totally unreconciled to her captivity, she snarled and spat at the approach of people. John Dominis had fenced her into a large area so that she could not escape while he was trying to work out ways of photographing her. So confined, she kept herself hidden most of the time in the densest part of the enclosure. Eventually her hunting instincts got the better of her animosity, and she would come out to stalk doves. She had the typical "fast hands" of a caracal, so fast that they could scarcely be seen in action. John was working with an automatic camera that clicked off an entire roll of 36 pictures in a few seconds, covering the caracal through the peak action of her attack. Although he made sequence after sequence during which she caught many doves, in the hundreds of exposures so made only two showed her actually striking a bird. One of those is reproduced on pages 174-175. In all the others the cat was simply too fast for the camera.

The caracal's close kinship with the cold-climate lynxes of North America and Eurasia is obvious in its tufted ears, its ferocity, its powerfully muscled body and in the length of the hind leg, which gives an unmistakable up-tilt to the hindquarters of all lynxes. The caracal differs from its northern cousins by being slightly more slender in build, as befits a warm-climate animal, in its spectacular russet coloring and in its greater length of tail. Northern lynxes have stumpy little tails and their coats vary greatly in color. Some have a faintly reddish cast to their fur, but most of them are gray or brownish, with a variety of markings, and a silvery grizzled look caused by the long white guard-hairs in their coats.

We come now to the truly small African cats. They are the least known of all —enigmatic little ghosts whose lives are full of gaps. They comprise five species, three of which overlap with races found in Europe or Asia, and two of which occur only in Africa. The largest—running up to 20 pounds in a big tom—is the jungle cat, an animal with a wide distribution from Asia Minor eastward through India and Ceylon as far as Burma. In Africa it is reported only from Egypt. I know it only from photographs, which show it to be an animal very much like a large house cat with longish legs and large slightly tufted ears.

Also from North Africa is the sand cat, the only feline in the world adapted to desert life. Until recently it was believed that there was another desert cat inhabiting dry wastes in Arabia and Asia Minor, but the two are now recognized as belonging to the same species. This animal is about the size of a house cat and has three interesting physical adaptations that fit it for desert living. Its coat is of a light sand color that blends well with its surroundings, paler and tawnier than a house cat's and showing fewer of the familiar tabby stripes on its legs. Its ears are larger than the domestic cat's, but instead of standing up high, they extend out to the side so that a straight line drawn from ear tip to ear tip would also almost touch the top of the head. This odd configuration is believed to allow the cat to peep unobtrusively over rocks while hunting, without exposing an unnecessary amount of ear. Furthermore, in a hunting animal with a small head, the widest possible separation between the ears could improve the binaural effect and thus serve as an advantage in the pinpoint location of small prey. The last peculiarity of this interesting little cat is that it has a hairy foot. Growing around and between the pads are clusters of thick coarse hairs that give the cat a better grip on the soft sand in which it is obliged to do much of its hunting. For survival, its principal prey—the jerboa, which is a small jumping-rodent resembling the kangaroo rat of the American desert—should also have hairy feet. It has.

Where the sand cat came from is not known. Five thousand years ago many areas of the North African desert were verdant land. The sand cat may have been living there then as a more conventional cat, and gradually may have taken on its present form and habits as the desert began to take shape. Or it may have become specialized for desert life at an earlier time in another place and moved into its present habitat only when conditions were dry enough to suit it. We tend to think of climates and landscapes as immutable. They are anything but that; only less immutable are the animals that inhabit them.

In dramatic contrast to the sand cat's habitat is that of the golden cat, one of the two small species found only in Africa. This is a forest animal, a denizen of that enormous belt of equatorial jungle that stretches across central Africa from the Atlantic Coast all the way to Uganda. The humidity in this region is high, the temperature constant. What winds there are die in the tops of the trees. Down on the forest floor it is silent and damp; the light is a deep-shadowed green during the day and as dark as a closet at night. Into this environment we must somehow fit the golden cat, which turns out to be a bit of a puzzle because the cat comes in two wildly contrasting color forms. One is a beautiful bright golden-red, shading to white on the belly. The other is grayish. As Armand Denis has pointed out, there should be some adaptive advantage for each color form, since they are so dissimilar. It is tempting to speculate that somewhere in that vast jungle there is an environment that favors the red form and another slightly different environment that favors the gray.

Unfortunately, from what scanty evidence exists about the distribution of the species, the two forms apparently live side by side with equal success. To cap the puzzle, and emphasizing how hopelessly inadequate our knowledge of some of these small cats is, there is the case of an individual in the London Zoo that changed from one color to the other.

Having disposed of the jungle and sand cats in North Africa and the golden cat in central Africa, we can move southward again to encounter the black-footed cat, the second of the two exclusively African species, and also the world's smallest cat. It is shy and believed scarce today, being found in the drier portions of South Africa and in the Kalahari Desert. It gets its name from the pads of its feet, which, unlike those of other cats, are invariably black. Otherwise it closely resembles the house cat in shape and coloring and is known to breed with it.

Since one of the classic tests of what makes a species is its inability to mate with other species to produce fertile offspring, does this suggest that the black-footed cat is the house cat's ancestor? On that evidence alone it would be logical to answer "yes," except that there is one more cat in Africa that also breeds with the house cat. This is the African wild cat. It is much more widely distributed than the black-foot, and for reasons that will be explained shortly, *it* is believed to be the house cat's ancestor.

Still, that does not dispose of the fact that house cat and black-foot interbreed. If they are able to do that, can they be called separate species? This question is best answered by examining what we mean by the word "able." There is physical ability and psychological—or behavioral—ability. In the wild state, members of different cat species do not naturally interbreed. They are too preoccupied with living their lives in their own particular niches to be able to afford the luxury of interbreeding. A leopard that approached a lion would not find a mate, he would provide a meal. It is only when the artificial ingredient of captivity is introduced that the rules begin to bend. Captivity has a profound effect on the behavior of predatory animals, for it relieves them of the crushing pressure of always having to find food and of regarding other predators as enemies rather than as associates. The removal of this burden expands their horizons. It lets them look around, as it were, to see and do things that in the wild state they would not do. A captive lion (i.e., one that has taken the first small involuntary step toward domestication) will mate with a captive leopard. So, by making captives out of wild animals, human beings can scramble matters considerably. They have, in effect, the potential to reverse the forces of evolution.

Whereas natural selection is constantly at work creating new species by intensifying the differences in structure and behavior between populations so that they will fit ever-more efficiently in their respective niches, captivity blurs the differences by removing the necessity to fit. A cat who is handed a meal every day on a plate not only does not have to compete with other cats of his own kind for his plateful of food—and thus does not have to pay the price of idiosyncratic behavior by losing out in his own "rat race" just as a nonconforming human might—but he can even afford to associate on entirely new terms with other cats. That is why the zoo lion and leopard will lie down together. And when they do they produce an odd-looking creature called a leopon. There are also tiglons (male tiger, female lion) and ligers (male lion, female tiger), plus numerous similar combinations among smaller captive cats.

Most of the big-cat hybrids are sterile, just as mules are, confirming that they are indeed the product of separate species. But with the African wild cat and the black-foot this is not so. Therefore, it is reasonable to suspect that their emergence as separate species is fairly recent, perhaps not yet complete, since their important differences seem to be more behavioral than physical. Today they could mingle to produce sexually viable offspring if only they would. What prevents them is partly geography (the black-foot inhabits a rather small and distinct range), but mostly inclination. Each prefers its own kind. As time passes and these preferences endure, a day will come when enough physical differences will have emerged in them, brought on by genetic change and intensified by natural selection, so that they too can no longer produce viable hybrid offspring.

Or, at least, that would be the story if it were not for the meddling hand of man. He has meddled with the African wild cat and out of that meddling produced a new species, the house cat. This species is only 5,000 years old at the very most and is still almost identical with its wild brother. Spiritually, it is its brother's brother through and through, for domestication has not changed the catlike nature of the domestic breed. The house cat is markedly self-sufficient and an excellent hunter. Abandoned, a house cat will quickly revert to the wild—and often live well. Even without abandonment it cherishes its independence. As any cat owner can testify, the most thoroughly home-oriented and affectionate tom or tabby may spend a good deal of time away from home on mysterious errands of its own, living a life that is a closed book to its so-called owner. "Putting the cat out" in a metropolitan suburb means exposing it to meetings with other domestic cats. In African villages one does not put the cat out—it comes and goes at will—but the effect is the same, with one important difference. When the mating urge is on the African domestic cat, it will go— and it will find wild cats (or black-foots) lurking nearby and will mate with them.

This keeps the African wild cat and the black-footed cat indirectly in touch with each other, genetically speaking, and to the extent that the house cat maintains these indirect links, it acts as a deterrent to the natural course of events by blurring the differences between the two wild species instead of permitting them to go their own ways toward greater and greater separation.

If we knew what the populations of wild cats and black-footed cats were, and if we knew the rate at which their gene pools were being invaded by house cats, we might be able to calculate to what extent, if at all, this meddling by house cats may affect the two species. But we know none of these things. We know only that the number of house cats is large, that this creature accompanies man wherever he goes, and that as man's numbers increase, the number of house cats will probably increase too. We know also—at least we may suspect—that the numbers of pure-strain African wild cats and black-footed cats are probably decreasing. As the land fills up with people there will be less and less room for the wild species to exist uncontaminated. Therefore, it is possible to look ahead to a not-so-distant time when the present species of wild cats and black-footed cats may become extinct—not by extermination, but through being engulfed by a wave of house-cat blood that so muddies up the differences that have been carefully building up in them over thousands of years that pure examples of the wild strains will no longer exist. That is evolution of a sort, but not the kind that would have occurred if natural selection had been left to work its will alone.

The modern house cat is itself something of a mixture. It is worth considering its origin—not only with respect to how it was first domesticated, but also where. How is not too hard to imagine. The wild cat is an extremely adaptable animal—probably the most adaptable and certainly the most numerous of any feline—with a range that extends throughout Africa, and large areas of Europe and Asia. Some scientists find three species and many races in this huge intercontinental population. A current view is that they are all really the same cat, *Felis silvestris*. Whatever its name and wherever it lives, it is irresistibly attracted to human settlements because of the excellent hunting found there in the form of rats, mice and domestic fowls. It can exist in close proximity with man because of its small size and furtive habits, and no doubt has done so for a very long time, tolerated around homes for its abilities as a ratter and mouser.

We know nothing about the actual steps taken by humans in domesticating the various animals that are now members of the human household, but in the case of the two predators—cat and dog—the process seems fairly clear. It almost certainly did not begin until after man had learned to cultivate crops and had changed his way of life from one of nomadic hunting and gathering to one of living in more-or-less settled communities. With the establishment of settlements came feeding opportunities for both the cat and the dog, and they took to hanging around. This, of course, enormously improved the chances for finding and raising kittens and puppies. The two influences taken together—the raising of pets and increasing familiarity on the part of wild adults—in time produced a strain of tame animals.

Where this first took place is not so easy to say. Small-cat fossils are known from prehistoric settlements in both Europe and Asia, but since the bones of tame and wild species are indistinguishable, there is no way of telling whether the fossils represent food or pets. The consensus seems to be that they represent food. The first solid evidence of domestication comes from Egypt. Some authorities believe that the Egyptians had pet cats as far back as 3000 B.C. It is certain that they did by 1500 B.C., for by that time pictures and statues of tame cats had begun to appear in tombs.

The cat had a unique position in Egypt. It was sacred to the goddess Bastet, or Bubastis, and was not only revered for its association with the deity but was also extravagantly admired as a pet. There was something inflammatory about the exposure of cat character to Egyptian character. Egyptians loved their cats with a passion. They went into mourning when their cats died and shaved off their eyebrows as a mark of respect. On their travels they went to considerable lengths to retrieve and bring home cats that they found in other countries. It was almost as if a cat could not be really comfortable or happy—or properly respected—outside Egypt. During the foreign occupations that were inflicted on Egypt during the days of her decline, if a visiting foreigner happened to kill a cat, whether by accident or maliciously, he was often killed in reprisal. When a cat died it was mummified and buried in a special cat cemetery, usually with its own bowl of milk to help it on into the other world. The number of mummies in these cemeteries is incalculable; the soil in some places is almost solid dried cat. Hoping to market some of this stuff as fertilizer, a merchant once shipped 19 tons of it to England. Reay H. N. Smithers, Director of National Museums in Rhodesia, has estimated that this one load, a mere sample of what is still in Egypt, contained the remains of 80,000 cats.

From Egypt the house cat made its way to Greece and Rome, and also eastward to India—ultimately around the world. Wherever it went, it inevitably mingled with the local populations of wild cats (and possibly with other closely allied species, as with the black-foot in Africa). As a result, the modern tabby is something of a blend. Domestication has done a few things to it. It is slightly smaller than its principal African progenitor, has shorter fur and not so thick a tail. Its legs are a trifle shorter, its face a bit broader and flatter. In coloring, both have the unmistakable "tabby" look, although the wild cat has a slightly rusty or reddish tint to the backs of its ears, whereas in the house cat these are almost always black-ish. Even so, and after 5,000 years of domestication, these differences are insignificant. It would be difficult, if not impossible, to state positively, by simply looking at and measuring a given cat, whether it was a largish tabby or a smallish wild cat.

If one had a chance to get acquainted, then some differences would become apparent, for the wild animal, when tamed or even when hybridized, retains certain behavioral characteristics that quickly set it off from the domestic breed. Stevenson-Hamilton once owned a hybrid male that had a wild tom as its father and a domestic tabby as its mother. This animal was friendly and docile, but did not like being handled, spent its days sleeping, was very active at night and an avid hunter. It mated with both wild and tame females, but its kittens, even by tame tabbies, were like their father. They would not tolerate handling either, spitting and scratching from the time they were old enough to do so.

Wild females are apparently more approachable than toms. For several years Reay Smithers has owned two that he got as kittens. Both are very fond of him and his wife, but they are not at all like house cats. For one thing, he has to keep them in separate enclosures, for they have strong territorial feelings, and the more aggressive of the two will drive the other away. Therefore they are let out in rotation. Before he learned this, one was driven off and lived in the wild for four months before she could be coaxed back again. Smithers describes as "humbling" his observation that although she had been raised as a pet she was still a superb hunter and came home in better physical condition than when she left. She had kittens by both wild and tame fathers. The former were generally unmanageable, the latter not. Five thousand years have clearly done something to soften the spirit of the house cat. That, more than physical change, is the evolutionary jump that has come with domestication.

INDEX

Numerals in italics indicate a photograph or drawing of the subject mentioned.

Akeley, Carl, and Mary L. Jobe Akeley, *Lions, Gorillas and Their Neighbors*. Stanley Paul, 1931.

Anderson, Sydney, and J. Knox Jones Jr., eds., *Recent Mammals of the World*. Ronald Press, 1967.

Astley Maberly, C. T., *Animals of East Africa*. Int'l. Publications Service, 1966.

Colbert, Edwin H., *Evolution of the Vertebrates*. John Wiley & Sons, 1955.

Corbett, Jim, *Man-Eaters of India*. Oxford University Press, 1957.

Cowie, Mervyn, *I Walk with Lions*. Macmillan, 1961.

Crandall, Lee S., *The Management of Wild Mammals in Captivity*. University of Chicago Press, 1964.

Denis, Armand, *Cats of the World*. Houghton Mifflin, 1964.

Denis, Michaela, *Leopard in My Lap*. Julian Messner, 1955.

Fey, Venn, "The Diet of Leopards," *African Wild Life*. June 1964.

"Fifty Thousand Leopards to Make Coats and Handbags," *Oryx*. April 1964.

Guggisberg, C.A.W., *Simba*. Chilton Books, 1963.

Haas, Emmy, *Pride's Progress*. Harper & Row, 1967.

Hallet, Jean-Pierre, with Alex Pelle, *Animal Kitabu*. Random House, 1967.

Hildebrand, Milton, "How Animals Run," *Scientific American*. May 1960.

Kruuk, Hans, "Hyenas, the Hunters Nobody Knows," *National Geographic*. July 1968.

Mannix, Jule, "We Live with a Cheetah," *The Saturday Evening Post*. March 12, 1949.

Martini, Helen, *My Zoo Family*. Harper & Brothers, 1955.

Molloy, Peter, *The Cry of the Fish Eagle*. Michael Joseph, 1957.

Muldoon, Guy, *Leopards in the Night*. Appleton-Century-Crofts, 1954.

Patterson, James H., *The Man-Eaters of Tsavo*. Macmillan, 1908.

Percival, A. Blayney, *A Game Ranger's Note Book*. George H. Doran, 1924.

Prater, S. H., *The Book of Indian Animals* (2nd rev. ed.). Bombay Natural History Society, 1965.

Roedelberger, Franz A., and Vera I. Groschoff, *African Wildlife*. Viking, 1964.

Roosevelt, Theodore, *African Game Trails*. Charles Scribner's Sons, 1910.

Schaller, George B., "The Serengeti Lion," LIFE. January 20, 1967.

Selous, Frederick C., *African Nature Notes and Reminiscences*. Macmillan, 1908.

Simpson, George Gaylord, *The Meaning of Evolution*. Yale Univ. Press, 1949.

Smithers, Reay H. N., "Cat of the Pharaohs," *Animal Kingdom*. February, 1968.

Stevenson-Hamilton, J., *Wild Life in South Africa* (4th ed.). Cassel, 1954.

Varaday, Desmond, *Gara-Yaka*. E. P. Dutton, 1964.

Zeuner, Frederick E., *A History of Domesticated Animals*. Harper & Row, 1963.

Significant contributions were made to this book by several people to whom I would like to express my gratitude. Joseph A. Davis Jr., Scientific Assistant to the Director of the New York Zoological Society, served as overall consultant. His careful reading of the manuscript and his many useful suggestions were enormously valuable to me. The evolutionary charts on pages 19 and 27 could not have been made without the help and advice of Richard H. Tedford, Associate Curator, Department of Vertebrate Paleontology, The American Museum of Natural History, New York City. The beautiful drawings on those same charts were made by Rudolf Freund. The pawprints scattered through the book were kindly supplied by Reay H. N. Smithers, Director of National Museums in Rhodesia. Finally, my thanks to Marjorie Pickens, staff research associate. Her long and careful labors on this book, from the time she began collecting research for the manuscript to the time the last proof went to press, have made a tremendous difference in its quality.

Maitland Edey

PRODUCTION STAFF FOR TIME INCORPORATED
John L. Hallenbeck (Vice President and Director of Production),
Robert E. Foy and Caroline Ferri
Text in 12 point Bookman, photocomposed under the direction of Albert J. Dunn
and Arthur J. Dunn
x

Design by Charles Mikolaycak